SATAN SOCIALISM AND THE DEMOCRAT PARTY

Richard Ferguson

SATAN SOCIALISM AND THE DEMOCRAT PARTY

What do they have in common?
PAIN AND SUFFERING!
Unfortunately, it's intended for you!

*A*dvantage
BOOKS

RICHARD FERGUSON

First Printing: January 2020
19 20 21 22 23 24   10 9 8 7 6 5 4 3 2 1
Printed in the United States of America

Introduction

There is a direct connection between Satan, socialism and the Democrat party. This book will explore the depth of these connections, how they were created, how they are bound together today, and the results of this sinful trio are made manifest in our country. Basically, it is the inherited sinful nature of mankind that Satan exploits in order to bring about his goals of the destruction of mankind including the children of God. Because of what happened so very long ago in the heavenly realm with Lucifer's rebellion against God, and later Adam and Eve disobeying God eating the apple of the tree of the knowledge of good and evil, we are saddled with a constant battle of good versus evil. This is the war that goes on inside all of our minds every day of our lives.

There is always a war going on in our lives between good and evil. It just never stops. We all have been born into this situation on earth. It is just part of living on this planet earth. There are times when good prevails and then over time it seems, the evil in us slowly builds up until there comes a critical point when it seems evil is running amok all around us. We are in one of those times today in our United States. Evil is running wild.

It is apparent to this writer that we have reached this point in our nation's history. I have observed the ever-increasing social unrest and violence in this country continue to increase over the last number of decades. The rule of law based on our Judeo-Christian foundations is now a target for godless leftist radicals openly attacking our country. They do this is so many ways. It is all based on hate, Satanic hate. We have sunk to new lows where even free speech and other bedrock freedoms that this country is founded upon are being attacked along with the people who exercise these rights.

Now because of the evil in our country, if you are a white person, you are automatically a white supremist, a racist and other horrible slurs that are hurled at you just because of your skin color. These thoughts are courtesy of the Democrat party who have been actively using "identity politics" to pit one race against another in the attempt to get votes. This is a famous and well-worn Satanic tactic. Barack Obama was a master of this and today after his presidency ended, we still are suffering from all the race-based hate he encouraged. How can a black president of this country ever think this country is racist? Is that not proof enough that whites are not racist. Muslim Obama never considered this logical thought. His hate is too great for that. He did these race-based attacks because of his agenda against America. He concentrated his activities to foment racial hatred while claiming our country is racist. More on this later.

When and how did all this race hate, sexism, all the invented phobias like, xenophobia, homophobia, sexism and other awful words used in our current political atmosphere come from? This did not just start recently. It did not start with Obama. It all started with Madalyn Murphy O'Hare back in the 1960's and before. I remember her well and the role she played fighting any display of our Christian God found in any place she did not want it to be. Madalyn was a rabid atheist. She did not believe in God and therefore she was determined to force her views on all of American culture and traditions. She brought many lawsuits against people and institutions citing the separation of church and state. If she could see a Christian cross anywhere, she automatically got offended and claimed the state was forcing a religion on the people. She was one toxic aggressive woman bent on removing any symbol of God from anywhere significant, even our classrooms.

One lesson our country is now learning. If you remove Almighty God from our public spaces, Satan will gladly enter, and show us how to further our own self-inflicted destruction. The farther a culture moves away from God, the worse things will become for those people. As an observer of our country for many decades I have witnessed this creeping destruction and how it has brought us to the situation we have today.

The latest love affair of the Democrats with a godless culture and socialism is a direct result of kicking God out of our public life. This is how we invited Satan into our society. We allowed the loonies in our country kick out God. Now we are seeing all kinds of perversions posing as freedom, so called rights given by our godless government to all forms of deviants now called the 'new normal". Thank you, Barry Soweto aka. Barrack Obama. Did you know that is his real name? Think about this and wonder why the Democrat Party and our media did not address this alias name before he ran for president. Manchurian for sure in my humble opinion.

The title of this book is "Satan, Socialism and The Democrat Party". There is a direct tie between these three entities. Satan, the author of all lies, is connected to Socialism. Socialism by its very nature must be against out Christian Almighty God. It is because that God must be gone from society for socialism to do its dirty deeds. For socialism to exist, a central all-powerful government that controls people's lives must rule the land. In socialism there can be no God. The state proclaims itself as god. God's children are stripped of their sacred sovereignty stolen by the state by force of arms and cheered on by Satan.

It is the Democrat party that wants to establish socialism in this country and solidify its position of power by encouraging no borders so more and more illegal aliens enter our country to ignorantly vote for Democrats. Most of these people are very vulnerable to socialist propaganda having no education. They do not know how a successful society should be guided. They will believe all the Democrat lies and vote accordingly. It is not through compassion Democrats want millions and millions of illegal aliens here. It is because they view these people as future Democrat voters.

In this book I will explore much information about Lucifer who became Satan our enemy of mankind and what his goals are against us. I will show how socialism is a government tailor made for the demonic rule of Satan over people and I will show how the Democrat party has been taken over by Satan and is now doing his bidding against the children of God in our country. To the extent that Democrats are successful in 2020, it is to that same extent that American citizens will lose.

Table of Contents

Part One

Our Judeo-Christian Philosophy/World View

A Loving Investigation:

I have a confession to make to you. I have done a lot of research on the Democrat party, their policy positions, their political tactics, their speeches, their history and their attitudes toward people. I have assembled a huge quantity of objective truth regarding Democrats and the leadership. I have paid a heavy emotional price and putting all this material together for your benefit. God has graced me with a hypersensitivity in all things including divine spirituality and being able to read the emotions of those in which I encounter in this life.

Being this way, by the will of God, I have discerned and analyzed the terrible evil that exists within the Democrat party. I have read multiple thousands of sources from many different writers and organizations that describe the actions the policies and the intentions of the Democrat party. I have paid a terrible emotional price because I cannot help but react as a loving child of God to the horrific cruelty that is exemplified within the Democrat party.

I want to emphasize to everyone however I'm speaking ONLY of the Democrat party leadership at all its levels. I am NOT speaking of regular people who happen to vote Democrat. I sympathize with these people because they do not understand what is behind the evil Democrat policies and what is ahead regarding the results of these policies if they are ever implemented against the American people. Normal loving people who are Democrat want the same things for themselves and their families as any other Republican or whatever beliefs a person may have.

The only problem is that for whatever reasons there are, many normal people have fallen prey to the lies and deceit that floods out of the mouths of the Democrat members of Congress. I do not blame anybody who is a normal American citizen because we are all so busy living our lives, raising our children and contributing to the health and well-being of our country. I do however completely condemn the evil that lurks within the hearts of the Democrat party leadership and its representatives in Congress. I believe that if these Democrat senators and representatives told the truth about what is really in their hearts and their minds, the American people would resoundingly reject them and kick them to the curb never to ever listen to them again.

I have been emotionally upset most of the time that I have written the trilogy of books that address the upcoming 2020 election. The first book is, "Christians Alert! Democrats are attacking our country." In this book I examined both the Republican and Democrat party. My overall conclusion in this book makes me sick to think that what I have written is true. Both parties are corrupt beyond belief. It only differs in the kind of corruption.

The second book in the trilogy is called, "The Children of the Swamp". This book is a direct result of my reaction to what Nancy Pelosi said in March 2019. She was reacting to something Pres. Donald Trump said about the vicious gang members in MS – 13. Pres. Trump called them "animals". Nancy Pelosi put on her Catholic wardrobe and her Christian sensibilities in order to condemn Pres. Trump by calling these vicious gang members "animals". Nancy Pelosi said that every member of MS 13 has a divine spark of God within them. She went on to further say that Pres. Trump is a terrible person for not recognizing the divinity of the gang members in MS 13.

Nancy Pelosi said that her Catholic Christian faith would not allow her to let Pres. Donald Trump get away with calling these vicious people, animals. She made it seem like she considered these gang members to be altar boys. They are not. They are the most vicious and cruel humans that occupy our planet earth. The articles that I read about what they do to other people was so upsetting to me, at times I felt like crying and puking. At times there were tears in my eyes reading and writing about what they have done to the people of from multiple news sources.

Nancy Pelosi is never to be trusted to tell the truth, especially in spiritual matters. She does NOT know or understand. She is completely ignorant regarding the theology of Christianity. The truth is that not everybody on this earth is a child of God.

Who We Really Are:

We are children of God. Our heritage is the heavenly realm and to that realm we shall return. We do not believe in the lie from Satan that human life is nothing more the result of accidental chemical reactions that have occurred billions of years ago and thus in essence have no lasting value and are essentially godless in nature. This is also why they hate anybody that has belief in Almighty God which is the antithesis of their theology of chemistry as the holy Grail for them than their alchemy of existence. I have a degree in chemistry/physics. I know we cannot be just an evolved bag of chemicals that somehow reacted and poof here we are.

Neo-Darwinists have hijacked the great scientific work done by Charles Darwin on the HMS Beagle many years ago. Darwin said that if it can be shown that an animal or other living thing cannot be explained by a series of small changes over a very long period of time, then his theory of evolution is wrong. I admire Charles Darwin for he was a great scientist. We have proven his theory wrong many times. Irreducible complexity proves it is wrong. In the first book of this trilogy, "Christians Alert! Democrats are Attacking Our Country" I cover this topic in detail. Darwin has been hijacked by evil minded Democrats that want to use his theory to cheapen the priceless value of the live Almighty God has bestowed to us His Children.

In my second book of the trilogy titled "Children of the Swamp", there are many people mostly Democrat who believe that we are truly nothing more than a bag of chemicals that has evolved over millions of years into what we see today. This is a complete satanic lie. However, most people in the Democrat party believe it.

Leaders of the Democrat party have no faith. They are lost children of Satan on earth that obsessively want dominion over God's children on earth and will do anything to get it. They are that filled with hate.

Faith, Knowledge and Reason:
In addition to divine love, it is God that wants us to have faith, knowledge and reason which in turn develops wisdom during our lives. This is fundamental to His design for human existence in this physical realm. Each one of the above supplements the others within the arms of our love for each other. There must be a balance of these three or human life will not live up to its potential for us as human beings.

God Has Said:

It will be faith that can guide you to the answers that mankind seeks. Faith is that invisible gift I give to those who humble themselves before Me in love and heartfelt sincerity. For in adoring Me, all my children will come to their highest fulfillment within themselves and grow into the beloved child I have ordained from the beginning.

The blessing of faith increases the inner desire of more faith. It is a pleasurable succulent warmth of having strong faith. For it engenders the inner desires of spreading faith to all brothers and sisters as they live in the world. It also engenders a need to learn knowledge of my creation, of the nature of all living things and the inner nature of my other children who are also living.

But, for those who choose to have only faith, they will cast their eyes upon Me in adoration and love. This is very pleasing to me. For it is those who have faith in Me that will be by my side after the world comes to its natural physical end. Yet for those who only want faith and do not pursue knowledge, they leave themselves less than whole. They fall short of my intentions for them for they have not understood that both faith and knowledge is the key for what they search for.

Only faith, although good and true, is like a one-legged man standing. A wind will come and blow his faith over and he will lose what faith he may have. Only knowledge is also a one-legged man standing. His other leg only will also succumb to the wind and blow him over. For only knowledge will never inform him as to why he lives, what direction he should take his knowledge and why one path is better than the other. It is with faith and knowledge guided by reason that you can pursue truth for truth is higher than anything else which also leads to wisdom.

Knowledge supports faith. Remember that faith supports knowledge. It gives knowledge a framework, a context in which to be meaningful. But, faith without knowledge is fragile, subject to the winds of confusion, to the opinions of the ignorant masses who have neither faith or knowledge. For they will have not used their powers of reason as well. Reason will in many ways link together knowledge and faith in Me the "I AM" of all creation.

I have given all my children the gift of desiring knowledge but also yearning for faith as well. Reason is also inborn with you as part of your natural being. Remember that when something good and right is desired, it is I that has given that to you. It springs from that deeply hidden part of you that is the closest to Me. It is in this way that I live within you and guide you to your complete potential as my beloved child.

I say to you the complete person fulfilled in all manner of being will have knowledge of my creation, faith in Me so as to understand why creation is the way it is and reason to make sound judgements, which leads to wisdom and choosing the divine path with love that I wish for each of you my dear children. Pursue all of this my dear children. Pursue these with all your might. For in doing so you will draw close to me as "I am" and fulfill the promise of the individual and priceless unique you I saw at the beginning of your existence within Me and outside Me.

Faith:

Faith is foundational to who we really are as human beings, God's children. Everybody has faith of one kind or another. All of us have faith that when we wake up in the morning the rules of physics haven't changed, we will wake up in the same place we went to bed, our existence has not radically changed and the world will still be here as we left it when we went to sleep. All of this is faith.

Atheists claim they have no faith. This is not true. Every human being walking the face of the earth has faith of one kind or another whether they even realize that themselves or not. Their faith is that God does not exist. Furthermore, their faith is that somehow through a mysterious mechanism unknown to anybody the cosmos just caused itself into existence. Somehow it followed physical laws that guided its development over 13.7 billion years into what we see today.

Stephen Hawking, one of the world's premier theoretical physicists, made a great blunder in 2010 when he said that the universe does not need God to explain its existence.

"Because there are laws such as gravity, the universe can and will create itself from nothing. It is not necessary to invoke God to light the blue touch paper and set the Universe going." [1]

He felt that the start of the universe occurred due to a random quantum fluctuation that got out of hand somehow. I believe Stephen forgot that all physical laws that he studies must have been in place before the universe started otherwise there would be

---

[1] The Grand Design, Stephan Hawking, Bantam Books, 2010

nothing to guide its development. Stephen Hawking's faith is in mathematics and human logic. I do salute his pure genius and wonderful intelligence, but he has limited himself without knowing it. Real faith goes far beyond just math and logic. It goes to the essential core of existence, both the seen and the unseen.

Faith is more than just adherence to a set of religious doctrinal and dogmatic beliefs. Faith goes beyond that. In a more general sense, faith is a firm belief in something for which there is no proof or can be no proof. It can be used as a synonym for the word trust.

You can say, "I have faith in her." Or, you can say," I trust her." Both sentences say the same thing within common understandings. When a Christian says they have faith, they mean they believe in and trust that biblical literature, and Scripture are true and accurate representations of the interaction between humans and God and God's son Jesus Christ.

Atheists on the other hand have faith that none of the Christian foundational truths are true. People of other faiths land somewhere in between with only partial understandings and acceptance of biblical truth. Yet the most important faith is the faith in God that is created us and loves us during every instant of our existence.

Knowledge:

God said there will be all too many of your brothers and sisters that will embrace the one only to reject the other. They will think that if they have knowledge there will be no need for faith. Knowledge of the physical is only part of a larger existence. Reason must be used to gain proper knowledge. It is this that will protect you from believing things that are untrue and lead you astray from your true spiritual path I have chosen for you. For if you increase your knowledge without faith in Me, you will falsely think that you do not need Me in your life. You will think that you are masters of your domain. You are not. For you will not know the infinite things that you do not know. This can only lead you to pain and suffering.

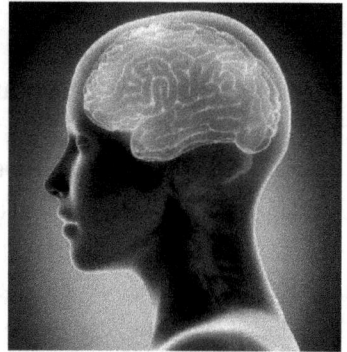

Knowledge by itself will only bring a dim light into the life of those who pursue only that. These people you will call scientists will never be able to answer the question of why all that is works the way it does. They will always have new questions and new thoughts in their personal blizzard of ideas that ultimately will lead them nowhere. The answers for these your brothers will only lead them to more questions.

The pursuit of only knowledge will ultimately bring them to the point of asking why things are the way they are. It is this question of why that brings one to the edge of faith. It is the search for meaning and asking where everything is going that is the beginning of wisdom. Wisdom comes from knowledge guided by reason and faith in Me. For knowledge by itself is only one arm. I gave each of you two arms. The other is faith. Knowledge is the arm of how. Faith is the other arm of why and of meaning. Reason is why you have a brain. Together with experiences in life in the physical realm yields the precious fruit of wisdom. And your heart of hearts in faith leads to Me. It allows you to learn about Me through the creation I have brought forth for you to understand and see Me as the painter that is behind His painting.

Reason:

I have given you the gift of reason. Some will call this logical thinking with objective observation. It is with you, so you may understand knowledge and use it for your betterment in the physical realm. Reason will guide you to understand many of the questions of "why" and "how". Then you must put effort into applying your knowledge for the betterment of all your brothers and sisters in the brotherhood of mankind.

If you use your gift of reason, you will link both knowledge and faith. It is this with my inner voice of what you will call conscience that will guide you and make clear the path to take. Remember that "I am" the truth above all.

It is reason that will protect you from making fatal mistakes in the physical realm. For reason combines perception and discernment and logical thinking to provide you with correct decisions which you will have to do each day of your physical existence.

It is past the open doors of my loving kingdom that you will be reunited with all that you have loved before. For that which you love becomes part of you. It is only through love that you can pass through the veils that are the doorways to higher and higher existence in the timeless place of infinite wonderment and joy that will remain beyond your understanding, at least for now.

What lays before you as you learn more deeply to love others is the kingdom of ecstasy. You will then be able to explore the other parts of my infinite creation. For there will be no time, no limits, nothing hidden. You will be able then to experience the lives of your brothers and sisters.

Wisdom

Wisdom is more than the combination of faith, knowledge and reason. The whole of wisdom is most certainly greater than the sum of its parts. Wisdom is a quality of both heart and mind. It is faith, knowledge and reason that when they resonate together within our loving inner being, they complete each other and support each other to form what we call wisdom.

Wisdom is not attained easily or by accident. It must be pursued with all your mind, all your heart, all your love, all your faith, all your knowledge and all your reason that when combined with a deep sincere love for all of God's creation then you will attain a wisdom that few have achieved.

Wisdom will allow you to see different things in their relationships between each other that will give you deep insight into that which appears before you. These insights will allow you to make loving judgments that will benefit your brothers and sisters in a much higher way and is consistent with the will of God for his children.

True wisdom is attained within a deep sense of humility and service to others. It lifts up a wise person to see the higher truths that exist well beyond the details of the here and now. Wisdom allows a person to apply the higher truths of existence to different situations and identify actions or that which is needed to be manifest and be consistent with the will of God. And also, it will allow you to reach intelligent conclusions that would escape others that have not sought faith, knowledge and reason and intermingle these three under the guidance of God our father. It is wisdom that will guide a child of God without the use of a map.

The Almighty's Objective Reality:

What is objective reality? First, there are two words in this term. The first word is an adjective, objective which modifies the second, reality, which is a noun. The definition of objective as an adjective means, "not influenced by personal feelings, interpretations, or prejudice; based on facts; unbiased".

The noun "reality" means, real things, facts, or events taken as a whole; state of affairs. Philosophically reality means something that exists independently of the ideas concerning it. something that exists independently of all other things and the minds that perceive it.

Combining philosophy, science and theology, the best way to think of objective reality is that it exists completely independent of the human mind and our perceptions of it. It does encompass everything that we can perceive and extends beyond that into everything that we are not able to perceive. Biblically speaking it is God's creation both the "seen and the unseen". Scientifically we know this is completely true as our senses are only able to perceive a very small amount of the electromagnetic spectrum.

Objective reality is also referred to as God's creation. Before God created our universe, which is another name for objective reality, a multitude of rules were set in place to govern the complete behavior of every aspect of both the seen and unseen objective reality. These "physical laws" operate regardless of our understanding of them, our perception of them whether we like it or not.

If we decide to disagree with the law of gravity for example and want to protest by jumping off a building, which is a behavior that many Democrat liberals might engage in, they will soon find out that gravity will accelerate their understanding of physical law. For, it is not gravity that kills, rather it is the sudden stop.

God's Keys to Success:

Almighty God has put before us is to be successful in this physical life on earth. Father in heaven is hidden nothing from us. We have no reason to complain about this. God told us that coming to earth would be a divine journey of our spirits. It would be a journey that had its challenges, full of hardships and sometimes pain and suffering, from others or ourselves.

My dear children, you will exist in the physical universe as the individual I created you as. But you will only be able to see your real self in the eyes of the other, not the one you imagine yourself to be. Yet there is a collective consciousness that you will share with all your brethren throughout all of eternity.

My dear children, I also give you my eternal guidance in your physical existence. I have made part of you, part of who "I am". In this way "I am" is always with you no matter where you are. In some ways you will call this conscience. I am your inner voice that guides you throughout all that you manifest, and all your choices set before you.

My dear children, I give you the freedom to set your eyes upon your unique path in life. Freedom to walk that path full of love, hardships, fulfillment, learning to love in different ways, being among your brethren and answering the big questions. My dear children, the freedom I give to you is something you can lose very easily. For only virtuous and loving people are capable of freedom. Freedom requires the loving control of one's own self.

My dear children I will give to you the ability to imagine that which does not yet exist. You will have the gift of creation in the physical realm, to bring into being that which is in your mind and manifest that in your world which is to come. You will have the freedom to choose the nature of that which you bring into existence.

My dear children, the question you will answer for all the universe and its inhabitants to see is what path you will choose. Will you love yourself first and put yourself above others or will you choose to serve them? Will you humble yourself in the sight of your brothers and sisters or will you seek dominion over them?

The Two Great Commandments: Mark 12:(28-31)

The first great commandment. We are to love God above all else with all our hearts, our minds and our souls. Put God first. Simple. The second great commandment. We are to love all others of Gods children as we love ourselves. In other words, we are all equal regardless of gender, race or all the other differences we may have. Also, simple. Both commandments are also elegant. All laws must necessarily follow from the above two commandments.

My dear children, the fruitful loving answer is to always remember to love Me your Father and Creator above all else, and love others as you love yourself. All good things come from these two great commandments. However, there is a great danger if you fail to adhere to these two great commandments I have put before you.

Lastly, if you fall in love with yourself that is all you will have in eternity. You will inhabit the darkness of only yourself with the light of my love not reaching you through your self-imposed veil that blocks out all that is good and right. You have the power to choose this path by manifesting and viewing yourself above others of your brotherhood, and in doing so you are placing yourself above Me. This is what the fallen one chose to do. You are wonderfully beautiful created as was the fallen one, but do not fall in love with your own beauty, that is a path my dearest children I warn you never to take.

All of this is part of the objective reality I have created for your benefit. This reality or creation is for your opportunity to grow into the magnificent spiritual being I have envisioned for each of you from the very beginning. I have created for each of you a loving path for you to follow so you can reach your own personal and individual sacred fulfillment. But like all of my children, I have given you free will. You can choose not to follow the path I have ordained for you.

The key is to love me first and love others as you love yourself. But if you fall in love with only yourself that is all you will have in eternity. You will inhabit the darkness of only yourself with the light of my love not reaching you through your self-imposed veil that blocks out all that is good and right. You have the power to choose this path by manifesting and viewing yourself above others of your brotherhood, and in doing so you are placing yourself above Me. This is what the fallen one chose to do. You are wonderfully beautiful created as was the fallen one, but do not fall in love with your own beauty, that is a path my dearest children I warn you never to take.

The Objective Summary of Reality:

The opposite of the will of God for his children on earth is loving ourselves above others of his children. The manifestation in this physical reality of loving ourselves above others is seeking dominion and control others. It is this singular phenomenon of dominion that has been the root cause of countless hundreds upon hundreds of millions of deaths of human beings and countless wars in our history. It continues on to this day.

Be aware of the person who seeks dominion over you or anybody else for that is the outward sign of evil in their heart and in their mind as perpetrated by Satan and his minions. If one takes the time to study the founding documents of the United States of America you will find that a very large portion of our Constitution and Bill of Rights is devoted to compensating for the evil tendencies of mankind and the desire for political power in order to achieve dominion over the people in our country. Power, especially political power, corrupts the soul of human beings like nothing else can. Money is another horrific corrupting influence. Politics bring those two things together like nothing else can and is a powerful corrupting agent that can bring out the absolute worst in people who are obsessively attracted to politics because inwardly they are sociopaths or psychopaths.

The laws of this objective reality known as God's creation work automatically no matter what we think of them. It matters not even if we acknowledge their existence. The laws of this objective reality work relentlessly 100% of the time and operate regardless of our opinions or our attitudes or any other nonrelevant emotion we may have regarding them. Just remember that gravity does not care what you think about it.

Therefore, the choices that you make in your life will produce consequences that are a direct result of what choice you make. The consequences of the choices you make in this life extend into eternity.

There is one property of this reality of both the seen and the unseen that almost everybody does not understand or is aware of. It is simply this. There is nothing in this universe. There is nothing in this objective reality that is unknown. 100% of everything, 100% of every detail of every circumstance and action is now by everybody and everything in this universe, in this objective reality. There is no such thing as secrets in this universe. Nothing is hidden from anybody at any time and at any place. Remember God is omnipresent. God is present everywhere. There is no place where God is not. St. Paul wrote about this in very loving terms and one of his epistles. Everybody must remember this. Even if someone is thinking about hiding something that fought in and of itself is known by this universe, by this objective reality that we call God's creation. Everything is known across the universe instantly. There's not even a time delay.

The Scientific Evidence Says This is True:

If you think this is too fantastic to be true, I will give you a scientific explanation. Within the last 20 years or so theoretical physics has performed experiments that have demonstrated something called subatomic particle entanglement. In nature particles are created in twos. They are entangled together to form a pair where if one spins one way, then the other particle will spin the other way. This keeps things balanced. Mother nature loves things that stay in balance.

Now, if we changed the spin of one of the particles, the other particle will also change its spin instantly. Now, here is the spooky part as Einstein has said. If we separate these two particles that are entangled a very very long distance and change the spin of one of these entangled particles, the other particle will still change its spin to compensate and it will do it instantly. Somehow the second particle knows that its partner changed its spin and reacts instantly no matter how far apart the two particles are and that communication between the two particles regarding the change of spin travels instantly at many multiple times the speed of light.

The point of all this is very simple. The communication of something happening to a simple subatomic particle that is entangled with another subatomic particle is communicated at speeds faster than the speed of light. And, we know from biblical literature God knows everything. He is omniscient and we now have a scientific experiment that is pointing in the direction that says the biblical statement is true. There truly is nothing hidden within this objective reality.

Like the old saying goes, the truth will always come out. The truth can never be hidden, ever.

Science Versus God:

One last related thought about science and God. There are many people who believe that if you believe in science you cannot believe in Almighty God. Conversely if you are a person of faith and believe in God then you must not be a believer in scientific thought, the scientific process and scientific discovery. Well, this is just plain BS. This is one huge false choice of Satanic origin.

To believe this is to be extremely evident about objective reality and Almighty God. The facts are simply this. God created objective reality. God created all the physical laws that govern the behavior of objective reality. Scientific investigation is the study of these godly created physical laws that govern the physical realm in which we live. There are also laws that govern the unseen world as well. Laws for example that govern the emotional world of human beings. Science calls that psychology. Science is learning about psychology and its effects on and because of human nature.

From all of my studies in my scientific background both in academia and at NASA and studies beyond that along with my studies in theology and pastoral ministry in graduate school I have come to the robust conclusion that science does indeed inform theology and theology does indeed inform science. In actual fact both these two areas of study are investigating two sides of the same coin. These two sides are not mutually exclusive. Rather, they are deeply connected together. They are very much entangled like card to subatomic particles above. Set a different way, science is the study of the laws of God the physical realm as he has manifested those for our benefit while we are here in this physical realm

What is Christian Philosophy?

What is our cosmic world view of existence?

To understand just how destructive to human life is with socialism, communism, oligarchies, dictatorships and other forms of non-free market democracies really is, we must review the foundational elements of the roots of these ideologies. We must determine which of these ideologies is the most productive and fruitful for human beings. We must understand how each of these ideologies work with human nature. Understand how they work with the rules and structure of this universe as it has been created by Almighty God. We must understand how these ideologies work with God's stated will for mankind extended all the way to each individual and each person's one of a kind uniqueness.

Whatever you do, don't be afraid of the word philosophy. There is nothing magic, mysterious or fatally boring about it. Whether or not you realize it, everyone uses philosophy at some point every day of their lives. They are just too ignorant to know that. This subject of philosophy is just not for dusty college textbooks taught by crazy wire haired professors with baggy pants that know nothing else. Understanding philosophy is actually necessary for success in life even if you call it something different like "life experience", "wisdom", "been around the block more than a few times" or "being grounded in reality". The manner in which you conduct your life is your personal philosophy of existence is another way to put it. Surprised? Don't be. You and everyone else is a philosopher and did not know that because you use philosophical principles all the time.

In order to understand the information in the remainder of this book more fully, a light introduction into philosophy is necessary. Knowing this will set you apart from all the other people in this world and it is a valuable tool that can connect things together for you that will bring more depth of understanding, meanings and insights to you that you would otherwise miss completely. This is absolutely great for making far better decisions regarding your life and your success.

Most people can only think as deep as the weathered paint job on a rusted out 1955 Chevy left in the sun for too long. One of my philosophy professors in college was famous for dressing down ignorant students by saying, "so, you claim that preposterous idea with your feet firmly planted in thin air." I am NOT going to review Socrates, Plato, Aristotle or Rene Descartes. So, let's go at least an inch deep into things and you will feel rewarded. All of it is actually understandable.

So just what is philosophy anyway? Different dictionaries say the following:

It is the study of the nature, causes, or principles of reality, knowledge, or values, based on logical reasoning. It is a system of thought based on or involving such study. It is the study of the theoretical underpinnings of reality or a particular field or discipline.

In other words, philosophy is the study of the unseen foundations or root causes and nature of why things are the way they are and how they work. It deals with the unseen part of God's creation. In a nutshell that is it. Simple actually.

One thing that is paramount in understanding thing like philosophy is that no matter what you study, science, mathematics, biology, astronomy, psychology, geology, philosophy and other intellectual topics, they are ALL based on a faith of some kind. There is nothing in this world that does not have faith or belief at its root and foundation.

What separates Christian philosophy from all the rest is that the core, the foundation and necessary faith is based on the revelations of Almighty God. Other philosophies are based and founded upon made up human constructs. It is this fact that puts Christian philosophy miles above anything else. Christian philosophy has the word of God as its foundation, the creator of all that is seen and unseen. The self-revelation of Almighty God is the root of all things Christian including its philosophy, its dogma, its teachings and principles of existence. This means among many other things, that Christian philosophy is in complete agreement and consistency with God Himself. This cannot be said for any other philosophy.

Christian philosophy is founded upon faith in the perfect word of Almighty God. Any other philosophy is based on human imagination. This fact alone dooms all of it to compete failure along with terrible pain, suffering and death.

Your demonstrated philosophy of life is how you conduct your life. Its your values, ethics (they are different), your relationship with other people, your patterns of thinking and reasoning, your logic and reason, what is important to you, your life goals, how you spend your time, your spiritual belief, your beliefs on what is your place on earth and actually the entire universe. All of this rolled up into the totality of you as a person is your philosophy of life. The fact that you are reading this book is evidence of your personal philosophy of life.

Christian Philosophy:

Christian philosophy is actually a very beautiful thing. It shows us how to live our lives to the fullest based on love for God, our neighbors and ourselves. It brings the light of God's love for each of us and frees us from the false and deadly promises of the dark side of life. This is why you see Christians smiling a lot while if you notice, Democrats do not smile that much and seem to be angry most of the time. Inwardly they know that they are on the wrong side of existence.

People who are angry much of the time are exhibiting signs of serious Satanic influence. It comes from the negative side of reality. Pray for them.

What is Christian Philosophy? It is based on biblical revelation, both the Old and New Testament. It spans across metaphysics, which is the study of our existence, epistemology, the study of knowledge, ethics, the study of morality and action and politics which is the study of human force over other humans. This differs widly from secular philosophies such as naturalism, materialism which are grounded only in the physical realm. Secular philosophies ignore the unseen spiritual reality that is actually far larger and far more powerful than just the physical stuff we encounter every day. Therefore, these philosophies are doomed to fail in the pursuit of increasing the health and well being of all of God's human children.

Christian philosophy requires faith in biblical revelation. The Bible does provide a rock solid philosophy of human life within the universe. Things are linked together very nicely with logic and reason. It is a very important subject because it ties together human existence with the spiritual realm that governs morality and guides us how to get along

25

with each other while living on this planet. I cannot go into great detail here for this is a topic that people spend whole careers studying. This would be a topic for another book.

In Colossians 2:8, St. Paul writes "See to it that no one takes you captive through hollow and deceptive philosophy. Paul describes the kind of philosophy he is warning against. It is philosophies which depends on defective human traditions and the basic physical principles of this fallen world rather than on Almighty God, Jesus Christ and the Holy Spirit. I can tell you now that the Democrat philosophy of life is an ugly fractured mess with crater sized holes, inconsistencies and leads people directly toward their eternal destruction. The philosophy of Democrat's secular philosophy is a direct descendent of Satan's hate toward Almighty God and His children. Democrat philosophy is based on materialism, envy, anger and hate for God and your fellow man. Its origin comes from the dark side of reality or in other words, Satan. Yes really!

Christian philosophy comes together based on love of God and your fellow man. Remember that this universe has an absolute set of rules that govern both the physical realm and the spiritual realm. It is "love for the other" that connects all things together for this is the will of God for all sentient beings in His creation.

Love is the glue that holds the entire universe together

It is God's love for each of us that led Him to create the physical universe. For it is only in the physical realm where we can learn and experience the necessary lessons and knowledge that prepares all of us for entering the glorious and far more beautiful higher realms of existence that extend far beyond what we can imagine today. The idea that Heaven is full of harps and clouds is completely false. You do not need to play the harp or even want to play the harp to enter the Heavenly realms. But you do need to have the capacity to love God and love others as yourself to advance into the unspeakably wonderous realms of what God has prepared for all of us if we live our lives according to his will.

Christian Philosophy – Faith, Knowledge, Reason and Wisdom

When it comes to Christian philosophy, the Bible does not in any way indicate to us that we must ignore our abilities to think, to make logical decisions or to blindly accept whatever it says. Islam does this because it seeks world domination as does Satan. It is much the opposite of Christianity.

"Come now," says the prophet Isaiah, "let us reason together, saith the Lord: though your sins be as scarlet, they shall be white as snow" (Isaiah 1:18). The apostle Peter encouraged all of us to present logical, compelling reasons for their hope in Christ (1 Peter 3:15). The universe has a set of understandable rules and principles that has been set forth by God. There is nothing beyond the heartfelt logic and reason of God's children. Because sacred things are understandable, God has provided us all a pathway to return to Him, to develop ourselves into higher and higher living spiritual beings that reflect and add to the sacred infinite creation of God.

Everyone at some point in their lives asks themselves about the important issues of our personal existence. What is it all about? Why am I here? What is it I should be doing? How should I spend my life? What does God expect of me in this life? How did I get here and not somewhere else? How can I make any sense of this life and why is it so very hard here on this earth? If God loves us so much why is there evil? Why does God allow evil? There are many more deep questions of existence that affect all of us.

For those people who are mature enough to ask these kinds of questions, they will find that Christianity does have answers to these questions. There is indeed NO OTHER BELIEF SYSTEM AND PHILOSOPHY THAT answers these questions more completely than Christianity. It shows why things are the way they are. It shows how things got this way. It shows how to prosper and grow into the full potential God has in mind for each of us. It shows the relationship and connections between the physical and spiritual realms.

Today the vast majority of people believe in a God, a fact St. Paul also found to be true in the Athens of his day (Acts 17:23). The challenge is to avoid the fake religions of today that are born out of the hateful mind of Satan. Islam is a very vicious and dark example of that. It is NOT a religion of peace as their advertising tries to make people believe.

Christian Philosophy – A Very Rational Foundation

Without going into much detail, Christian philosophy sees no conflict between the physical realm and the spiritual realm. The popular issue of "is it science or God". I find that to be a very stupid question. God created the physical realm for us. Science is the study of the laws of the physical realm. They are NOT mutually exclusive. Science is much like studying a painting so as to learn more about the painter. Science is a wonderful pursuit as it will ultimately lead to the Bible and Almighty God.

Science that you have been taught in school involves rock solid laws of physics like gravity, equal but opposite forces like momentum and inertia, force equals mass times acceleration and many things like that which govern our everyday lives. It all involves linear thinking and are logical to the human mind and our perception of the world. This is called Newtonian physics. The laws that govern big things.

The branch of physics that explores the subatomic world on the other had has NO linear thinking involved. It is called quantum physics and it explores the nature of reality beginning with the subatomic level, the world of particles that make up atoms. It deals with probabilities for positions of electrons, and probabilities of either this or that happening. Nothing is certain, nothing. Everything is governed by probabilities.

It is only recently that science has progressed far enough to discover that there is an inexorable and tight connection between human consciousness and physical matter. In actual fact what appears to us as physical matter is actually "condensed energy". Matter that we think is solid is NOT. It is actually almost pure empty space. If a nucleus of an atom was the size of a baseball, the nearest electron would be 20 miles away with nothing in between except empty space and magnetic forces between the protons and the electrons.

Quantum physics proves that like the unseen laws of spirituality, matter is actually packets of energy that cannot be seen either. If you were to hold that same baseball in your hand, at the sub-atomic level, it is not solid at all as you perceive it to be. Rather it is a complex arrangement of atoms very far from each other where each part of the atom like protons and electrons are actually packets of condensed energy with only probabilities of being somewhere here versus there. Surprisingly, if it were not for the force of electromagnetism, because of the large distances between an atom's nucleus and its electrons and the space between atoms, you could walk through walls. Everything would be permeable. Quantum physics describes this nature of the root essence of matter which is energy and the fundamental forces of what makes the physical world, condensed energy packets which give rise to what we call matter.

Everything in this universe is energy, some condensed and some not. Matter is condensed energy into packets of discreet amounts. Light is a duality of both wavelengths of energy and packets of energy called photons. Other kinds of energy are only wavelengths such as infrared energy we call heat. Just remember that everything in this universe is energy in one form or another. This leads to an astonishing conclusion. There is nothing solid in this universe including you and me. We are all inexorably connected because everything including you, me, the furniture you are using right now etc. are made of the same energy.

"In short: everything is energy, energy influences other energy, and energy appears out of thin air. What this means is that since we are all energy, we are all connected. Matter does

not separate us because—we are not matter! You and I have a whole lot more in common than you think…we are actually connected!" [2]

What are you and I made of? It goes something like this. Each of us are made of flesh and bone. Our flesh is made of different kinds of organic cells each with a different job to do. Each cell is made up of a myriad of different complex "factories" that perform different functions like using glucose to make the energy we need to live. Each factory is made up of different chemicals and arrangements to perform different jobs. Each chemical is made of a number of different molecules. Each different molecule is made of different atoms like hydrogen, oxygen, carbon etc. Each atom is made of protons, neutrons and electrons. Each of these subatomic particles are made up of different combinations of quarks. Each quark is made up of one dimensional strings. Each of these strings vibrate at different frequencies that determine the nature of the individual kinds of quark. Each string is indeed one dimensional and is actually energy vibrating at different rates. So, the bottom line is that everything physical is actually made of vibrating energy strings that determine its fundamental nature. Conclusion: everything is made up of energy with different frequencies of vibration. We are all made of the exact same kind of energy stuff.

"But when you become aware of and combine the underlying conclusions that Quantum Physics reveals, with what the mystics, sages, masters and philosophers since antiquity have to say about life and how our lives come to be the kind and quality that they are, (whatever that entails) is not only PROFOUNDLY exciting, it CAN prove to be the catalyst that transforms your entire life." [3]

Lastly regarding the ultimate basic nature of reality is well described here:

"A fundamental conclusion of the new physics also acknowledges that the observer creates the reality. As observers, we are personally involved with the creation of our own reality. Physicists are being forced to admit that the universe is a "mental" construction. Pioneering physicist Sir James Jeans wrote: "The stream of knowledge is heading toward a non-mechanical reality; the universe begins to look more like a great thought than like a great machine. Mind no longer appears to be an accidental intruder into the realm of matter, we ought rather hail it as the creator and governor of the realm of matter." [4]

All of this makes perfect sense once you realize and consider that our entire universe at one point in time at the big bang of creation, there was nothing but energy in existence

---

[2] https://truthofself.com/what-does-quantum-physics-have-to-do-with-spirituality-everything/

[3] http://www.abundance-and-happiness.com/quantum-physics.html

[4] R. C. Henry, "The Mental Universe"; Nature 436:29, 2005

and the Godly defined laws that governed the characteristics and laws of our universe as the big bang cooled down yielding matter and other phenomenon.

What Does This Mean? [5] [6] [7]

Christian philosophy and worldview understand the above and modern scientific understandings are incorporated into Christian thought. With the above scientific explanations in mind, now consider the miracles described in Biblical literature. You will now see these miracles in a completely new and different light where what you thought impossible is now far more reasonable. Now you can see that the possibilities of the strange things described in the Bible are far more likely, far more reasonable and widespread.

Even within Buddhism we find the following:

"Broadly speaking, although there are some differences, I think Buddhist philosophy and Quantum Mechanics can shake hands on their view of the world." – The Dalai Lama

I am happy that the Dali Lama expressed this thought. However, Buddhism is very incomplete in that it does not recognize Almighty God and the fact that God's creation includes both the physical, the spiritual and the sacred laws that govern both realms. In my opinion Buddhism is more of a philosophy of life then it is a religion.

While Marxists, which include socialists, communists, Muslims and secular humanists, look to science as the primary source of human knowledge, they completely fail to include and understand the true nature of reality that does include Almighty God as the true source of reality and knowledge. These bankrupt ideologies fail miserably to explain reality in any ration manner. Rather they are forced to deny and or ignore the truths set forth by Judeo-Christian principles that include both the physical and spiritual realm. They cannot demonstrate the source of all truth. Thus, they all are doomed to complete failure and bring only pain, suffering and death to humankind. The history of these man-made ideologies prove that they are complete failures that do not in any way enhance the health and well-being of God's children on earth. Rather, they produce just the opposite where the vast majority of the people suffer greatly and experience the equality of abject poverty while being controlled by an elite class people associated with

[5] http://www.abundance-and-happiness.com/quantum-physics.html
[6] https://www.ncbi.nlm.nih.gov/pmc/articles/PMC4217602/
[7] https://www.collective-evolution.com/2017/04/26/dalai-lama-spirituality-without-quantum-physics-is-an-incomplete-picture-of-reality/

government that lead luxurious materialistic lives while controlling every aspect of the regular population and their lives.

Christian Philosophy – All Philosophy Requires Some Faith

Christian philosophy does not reject reason or tests for truth. Christianity says the New Testament is true because its truths can be tested. Christians do not ask non-believers to put their faith in a revelation of old wives' tales or fables, but instead to consider certain historical evidences that reason itself can employ as an attorney building a case uses evidences in the law to determine questions of fact. Christian epistemology is based on special revelation, which in turn is based on history, the law of evidence, and the science of archaeology.

Philosophical naturalists also make assumptions that they, by definition, accept on faith. All naturalists agree that there is no supernatural. "This point," says Young, "is emphasized by the naturalists themselves without seeming to be at all troubled by the fact that it is an emotional rather than a logical conclusion."[6]

Faith is critical in every philosophy. When developing a philosophy, we must be extremely careful to base our case on the most truthful assumptions—otherwise, should one of the assumptions prove to be untrue (as it appears the assumptions of the theory of evolution will be), the whole philosophy will crumble. If evolution crumbles (which is quite possible—Dr. Karl Popper believes evolution does not fit the definition of "a scientific theory"), Marxism and Humanism are intellectually dead.

So far, we have established two things regarding Christian philosophy: many hold it to be the most rational of all worldviews, and it requires no more faith than any other philosophy. Indeed, we could argue that it takes a great deal more faith to believe in the spontaneous generation of Darwinian evolution or the randomness of all nature (i.e., that the universe happened by accident) than it does to accept the Christian doctrine of Creator/Creation.

The Christian Philosophy/Worldview: [8]

In general, a world view is a set of beliefs and assumptions that are used to provide a framework in understanding the world. Everybody does have a worldview whether they think of it or not. Said a different way, a worldview is the lens of thought, belief and assumptions through which we see the world. In a real sense looking through the lens of your worldview shapes how you interpret the reality we live in.

---

[8] https://carm.org/what-are-some-christian-worldview-essentials

There are good and productive lenses and there are bad and destructive lenses. Every worldview does have assumptions built into its foundations. For example, if you have a materialistic worldview, this means that things that you assume there is nothing else in existence that extends beyond the physical, are unseen are unimportant to your life. It means there is no God. It means that the only things of value in this life are those that can be seen, felt, tasted, heard and smelled. It is a worldview where your senses are the only thing that you interact with the world. Nothing else is important. I tell you sincerely that there are many people with a materialistic philosophy and worldview. This kind of thing is extremely primitive in nature and is an insult to the loving potentiality of God's children living on this earth.

The Christian worldview is largely shaped by the following:

1. There exists Almighty God that is all powerful, infinite, loving, is infinite is complete in and of himself, needs no external cause for his existence, and is eternal.
2. Man is created in the image of God
3. If man is created in God's image, we are therefore worthy of respect and honor as children of God
4. Each of us children of God are a one of kind unique individual. There are NO duplicates of any of us.
5. We are all born into this world unique spiritual beings and into different circumstances, some better than others
6. We as children of God are eternal spiritual beings. Where we go after earth is defined by our attitudes and actions here on earth.
7. God created the universe we live in. God created all that is seen and unseen.
8. God gave mankind dominion over the earth
9. There is evil in this world because Lucifer, the morning star, fell in love with only himself and inequity was found in him. He rebelled against Almighty God therefore falling out of grace and was expelled from the heavenly realm. He became Satan and now he wants to destroy all of God's children made in the image of God. He is the prince of this earth. This is why there is evil in this world
10. Through our ancient parents Adam and Eve, mankind has fallen from grace due to gaining the knowledge of good and evil. They disobeyed Almighty God. It is Satan that tempted Adam and Eve to disobey God and they did so causing the current battle between good and evil on this earth. Mankind now has a distinct tendency toward sin and corruption.

11. Because of Adam and Eve gained the knowledge of good and evil, mankind does not now have the ability to fairly and justly govern itself.

12. The power of governance surely corrupts those who gain political power

13. Jesus Christ, the only begotten son of Almighty God, came down to earth to redeem God's children from the penalty of death for their sins against God

14. The word of God is contained in our biblical literature. It contains God's guidance how we should live our lives and therefore return to God's heavenly kingdom

15. God loves every one of his children and he provides for us and all his creation and sustains the existence all his creation.

16. God has given mankind the keys to his heavenly kingdom. These keys are called the 10 Commandments. Of these 10 commandments there are two great commandments which the rest are derived from. These two great commandments are: [9]

    a. [37] Jesus replied: "'Love the Lord your God with all your heart and with all your soul and with all your mind.' [38]This is the first and greatest commandment. [39]And the second is like it: 'Love your neighbor as yourself.' [40]All the Law and the Prophets hang on these two commandments."

17. We are all here on earth for a sacred reason ordained by God. We do not necessarily know all the individual reasons that each of us are here. But these reasons exist. And they are related to our spiritual growth in our eternal spiritual journey of which living on this earth is only a part. How we live our lives on this earth will determine which direction our existence goes to next after we leave this earth.

The above points constitute in general the Christian world view. It is through the lens of these points that Christians view this world and everything in it including all human action. It is this lens that puts into perspective our lives and our existence within God's creation.

There are assumptions with this worldview as well. Christians assume for example that we have the gift of being able to perceive God's existence living on the earth. We assume that biblical texts are understandable in a correct way by us humans. That we have the intellectual power to do so. There are more assumptions and going deeper into this topic would require me to write another book.

---

[9] Matthew 22:36-40 (NIV)

The Philosophy of Free Market Enterprise:

The free market enterprise economic system is completely compatible and consistent with the Judeo-Christian worldview of physical and spiritual reality. This is one very significant and hefty statement loaded with truth and shines light on the best way in which mankind, through the guidance of God Almighty, has discovered to increase to the maximum our health, wealth and well-being physically, morally and spiritually.

Competitors

Free Market Economy

Free market enterprise is consistent with the nature of mankind. God bestowed within us a yearning to always make things better than they are. This is an act of love for not only ourselves, but our families and those people around us. If I have an idea to make a widget that will for example allow people to communicate over long distances any time they wish and no matter where they are that would be a wonderful thing. People would buy something like that so they can talk to their friends and family anytime they wish. A person providing such a device should be rewarded handsomely in the marketplace by people purchasing the device and using it to increase the quality of their life. You just heard the story of Apple's iPhone.

The inventor was free to create a wonderful device for communicating. If the device satisfied the wants and needs of other people they were free to purchase it on the open market. If they didn't want to purchase it, they didn't have to. Here is a key point. It required capital, money and other words, to invest in the research and development and production of this communication device we call the iPhone. They country must have enough wealth to fund entrepreneurs creating more wondrous things for us to purchase that increase the quality of our health wealth and well-being. And as consumers we get to choose which kind of iPhone to purchase. A company is only rewarded if they provide the goods and services people want. If they can do that, they go bankrupt and out of business.

God has intended us to be free evidenced by the fact he has gifted to us free will. And, we are free to purchase one kind of iPhone or another or none at all. We take this for granted and think that this kind of system will "always be here". Smart mouth idiot Democrats do not realize that socialism will destroy the potential for creating more inventions like iPhones in the future. This is because there will not be the necessary capital to invest in the research and development and production of the new products. As a result, the quality of life and the health and well-being of people will decreased dramatically.

Cuba and Venezuela are the poster boys of socialist failure on a global scale. Historically we can see that China, most African countries and Russia are still mired in trying to control economies from a central government which is always and 100% of the time doomed to failure.

Being able to choose which products you wish to purchase in a free market economy is the most consistent with the will of God because again, he gave us free will to allow us to co-create ourselves with the guidance of God Himself.

Satan hates this kind of freedom for God's children. He'd lusts for dominion over the lives of God's children. Providing us with many choices in the marketplace for the goods and services that will address our needs goes directly against the evil control, the central dominion of Satan that he so very much lusts after. This is why Satan's children on earth push so hard for socialism because it manifests the evil central control over God's children on this earth.

A Huge Problem:
In any culture or society there is the constant problem of "keeping things going". Meaning that a culture must be taught to the children. Otherwise, they will have to start from zero again and not benefiting from the collected wisdom of previous generations. This is what has happened with the baby boom generation. We DID NOT teach our children the reasons they live in the best country mankind has ever created, (with God's help of course).

Our Culture, Democracy and Society is Only One Generation Deep:
Free market capitalism and a democratic republic form of government has been the keys to success for the United States of America since 1776. We revolted against King George in England then refused to remain just a colony of the British Empire who took economic advantage of us.

We have a marvelous heritage, not a perfect one but a heritage that has broken all records for promoting the health and well-being of its citizens. We have become the world's only superpower and that is unquestioned. Be very happy that you are living in the most successful country world is ever produced as it was guided into the hearts of our founding fathers 240 years ago by Almighty God. White Europeans succeeded in creating a country that is inspired by being consistent with the sacred will of God for all his children. It is this close alignment with God's rules for human existence that has propelled our country to be the best country ever created by mankind.

However, nothing stands still in the world is constantly changing. We as American citizens must actively participate in educating our children and our children's children about the keys to cultural success, Almighty God's creation and his rules for existence. The United States is successful because we are the one nation on planet Earth that has successfully implemented God's rules for life in our Constitution and our Bill of Rights. I do not give a damn if the Democrats do not like this but the fact of the matter is regarding human existence and human fulfillment and success, it is those people that adhere to the rules of God for his children that will reap rich rewards in health, well-being and fulfillment while they are living this life on planet Earth. Following the rules of God diligently also dramatically affects a positive outcome regarding where each of us will spend eternity after we leave this planet we're on.

Our founding fathers have structured our government in such a way as to compensate for the dark side of human nature as best we can. However, there is one glaring and destructive fault that the baby boomer generation and to a lesser degree the one behind has committed. It's that we have failed in our responsibility to fully educate our children and our children's children on how to preserve and improve our democratic republic and our form of free market capitalism.

Instead we have passively allowed ideologues and left-wing idiots corrode our education system. It is these people that wish to destroy the best and most successful Christian nation the world has ever seen. From a theological perspective who do you suppose is behind this? Who do you suppose is the spiritual entity that hates God the most because he was thrown out of heaven for his lost for power and dominion? The answer is easy. It is Satan and Satan's minions who were tossed out of heaven with him.

For reasons unknown to me there appears to be an affinity between Satan, Satan's tactics of lying, half-truths, attacking God's children, innuendo and out right hate and the attitudes and tactics of the Democrat party.

It is at the point now where college is more of a four-year indoctrination than it is an education on how to think, how to reason, how to apply logic and problem solving, how to understand the physical world around us and how to understand each other in loving ways. My generation has failed miserably at this. And there is no shortage of socialist brain dead idiots that have flocked to our education system in order to indoctrinate our children against the very principles and morality that has made this country the greatest country in human history.

"I think Ronald Reagan was right when he said we're always one generation away from losing the freedoms we currently enjoy. Along with the siren song of socialism, the persistent promise of 'free' stuff, and the breathtaking level of censorship on our college campuses, I worry about the growing belief among many that we can somehow improve our present by erasing our past; by toppling statues, outlawing 'problematic' symbols, or rewriting specific pieces of our history in ways that leave us feeling less offended." Mike Rowe

The Philosophy of Socialism and Its Destructive Power:

Definition of socialism:

Socialism is an economic and social system that advocates a completely classless society. The very large central government controls everything. This means it controls the means of production, the distribution of goods and services. In most cases the government owns everything including all factories, all companies, the distribution of food and other goods and even the house you live in. There is no private property. You cannot own your own house. The government controls all wages, benefits and income. The goal is to make everyone just like everybody else. Communism is socialism

NATIONAL SOCIALISM   DEMOCRATIC SOCIALISM   MARXIST SOCIALISM

Change!   CHANGE!   СНДИГЭ!

In troubled times, the fearful and naive are always drawn to charismatic radicals.

on steroids. The idea is that if everyone works, everyone will reap the same benefits and prosper equally. Therefore, everyone receives equal earnings, medical care and other necessities.

Socialism says that everybody is the same in all things. This Completely Violates God's Natural Laws

The best way to picture a life like this is to go back to your childhood. You are living with your parents. They control everything about your life. You get an allowance to buy little things you might want. You go to school everyday which you did not choose. All decisions about your life is made by mommy and daddy. This is socialism. But you are an adult now. Your parents are not the government. The government replaces parents and controls every aspect of your life. Decisions about your life are made by invisible bureaucrats who don't even know your name. This is the face of socialism.

The underlying philosophy of socialism and the Democrat party includes the following morbid points.

1. Everyone is equal in every way. Nobody is deserving of anything more than everyone else. The individual as a unique spiritual person does not exist. All our needs are the same.

2. If you are born with more natural abilities than others, you are NOT to benefit from that because that would be unfair to those without those abilities.

3. Each person is entitled to the production created by all others. This is only fair

4. No person can have more wealth than another. This would be unfair and unequal.

5. Wealth redistribution is fair and just to ensure equal outcomes

6. There is no Almighty God. God does not exist

7. Mankind is the ultimate sovereign over all life on earth

8. Mankind is fully able to govern its own population and creating societies rules

9. Life started on earth by an accidental chemical reaction. Over billions of years and chance chemical reaction more complex life forms evolved. Mankind evolved out of primordial slime through the process of random selection and survival of the fittest.

10. All life is from a complex series of chemical reactions. This includes human beings. There is nothing more than this.

11. There was no divine creation of this universe. The universe created itself.

12. People are basically good

13. There is no life after death. Life and consciousness are only a product of biochemical reactions. Death means annihilation forever, oblivion.

14. Humans are just another form of life on earth. We are just another animal.

15. There is no absolute objective truth. Everything is relative, therefore there can be no real natural law

16. Pleasure is a high goal, even at the expense of someone else

17. No one, no single person is priceless. Your value depends on your role in society

18. Principles and values are changeable over time

19. Morality may differ between two people, there is no absolute morality. What is right & wrong for one person may not be right & wrong for another. Both are acceptable.

20. It is okay to separate human beings into different groups and classes each with different human rights. Some races are politically better than others. This changes with time as Democrat party history shows without a doubt.
21. The end does indeed justify the means. Honesty and morality are flexible when you factor in what the goal is. Morality is flexible as in number 18.

Not one Democrat that you can speak with including the leaders of the Democrat party will be able to articulate the above foundational philosophical points that they believe in. Democrats do not think that deep. They live on the appearances of things only. This is because and it is fair to say that Democrats play it by ear. Meaning what feels good at the time and seems it's probably politically advantageous is what they will pay attention to in defining government policy. They are absolutely terrible in foreseeing the consequences of their policies. This is why you will never hear the term "Democrat forecaster". This term is an oxymoron. Democrats that can or want to see in the future regarding the effects of their policies are as scarce as hen's teeth. For those of you who have never lived on a farm that means it doesn't exist. It is fair to say that Democrats are driven only by emotion and not any form of analytical thought or consistency in their thought patterns. They all tend to react according to their emotions without any sort of objective evaluation.

Republican president Richard Nixon used to have a saying regarding whether or not to adopt a particular political position. He would always say," how will it play in Peoria?" In other words what will the people think. This is very much like the Democrats of today in that they take tremendous efforts to market and sell their proposals with candy coating all around them to make them look good when they are actually not. Democrats only deal with the appearance of things and not the deeper inner issues of human existence and what is best long-term for God's children.

Summary Existential Philosophy of Democrats:
Sadly, when analyzing and thinking about the above principles of socialism and the Democrats I do not find any eternal unchanging principles of existence that they base their politics and policies on. When looking at each of the above principles it is striking that they are all changeable based upon the political climate with a few unavoidable exceptions.

These exceptions are the complete denial of the existence of God or at least they consider him a royal pain in the ass and to be ignored. A human being is not considered a unique individual person. We are all only a collection of chemicals with a head two arms and two legs. Our identity in only in relation to what we are in the community. Lastly there is no real morality. That changes with the times and differs from person to person. This is a complete denial of the reality we live in as created by Almighty God.

The rest of their so-called principles can be changed based upon the next polling results. This is completely proved by what Lyndon Baines Johnson did in the late 1960s in the civil rights Bill. Before that the Democrat party was the party of black slavery. After decades of fighting against Republicans who wanted full rights bestowed upon Blacks they finally gave in and became a highly destructive force against Blacks while painting themselves as black people's savior. If you think this is not true, I will tell you from personal observation over the last 60 years that black people are economically just as worse off as they were in the 1960s even after spending what must be by now trillions of dollars on the black community led by Democrats.

I feel so very sorry for our black brothers and sisters who are caught up in the trap of Democrat social programs and rotten schools like those that exist in every Democrat controlled city in the United States like New York, Chicago, San Francisco and Portland and Seattle and the list goes on. It is my opinion that the Democrat party is in reality not at all interested in permanently solving the problems that continue to afflict major parts of the black community. The evidence is very simple, the Democrat party is completely against school vouchers. This would allow black kids to get a far better education. This is what the Democrats are completely against this because they know it would **break** the cycle of poverty. Democrats view the black community as a reliable voting block that Pres. Johnson foresaw 50 years ago. If you have the money and wish to do something very good for a black child, pay for their education in a good school. This is something that Booker T Washington has said a very long time ago. It was obvious then and it's obvious now.

A Democrat Party Motto:

Never let a Godly divine loving principle stand in the way of political success. It's dominion we want and dominion we will get!

Are Democrat Principles Above in Agreement with The Will of God and the Structure of Creation?

NO! They are actually opposite! When comparing the above, Democrat principles and the principles of Christianity it is easy to see that they are adamantly opposite of each other. The great commentator Paul Harvey years ago talked about what he would do if he was Satan. When looking at the Democrat principles and their proposed policies if they get elected in 2020, we see the same list of Satan's action items very much as what the Democrats want to do to us if given the chance. It is not a coincidence in my view that the Democrat party promotes the very same destructive policies and principles that Satan would use to destroy all of God's children here in the United States. I refer to the section on Paul Harvey.

Part Two

Understanding Satan Is Very Important

Many People on Earth Are Children of Satan! [10] How "The Hell" Did That Happen?

If you count, there are 97 versus in the Bible, both Old and New Testaments, that directly addresses Satan and his children on this earth. The footnote above is a link to a site that has all of them. Here are just two.

And the great dragon was thrown down, that ancient serpent, who is called the devil and Satan, the deceiver of the whole world—he was thrown down to the earth, and his angels were thrown down with him. Revelation 12:9 ESV

You are of your father the devil, and your will is to do your father's desires. He was a murderer from the beginning, and has nothing to do with the truth, because there is no truth in him. When he lies, he speaks out of his own character, for he is a liar and the father of lies John 8:43 ESV

Everyone must understand that there are 97 different verses in both the Old Testament and the New Testament regarding Satan on earth and his children. They are the enemy of God's children and manifest themselves in many different ways. As a person with a graduate degree in theology I can tell you with authority that because of certain events that occurred in our far ancient history some of the demons of Satan had children with human females. This started an ancestral tree that has produced over

---

[10] https://www.openbible.info/topics/satans_children

the many years many children of Satan. They look like you and me but have Satan in their heart, not God. I invite you to please do your own research on this topic. You will find it most informative and upsetting. But please remember the biblical sources involved are true because it is indeed God's word to mankind.

So, every Christian must remember that everyone you see walking down the street or in any social interaction are not all God's children. Many of them are children of Satan and his demons. They walk the streets with us every day. But do not be afraid for a tree is known by its fruits. A child of Satan will be known by what they say and do and the fruits of what they create on earth.

There was a war that started in heaven and untold amount of time ago. And now that war continues within the spiritual realm which intersects with the physical realm on earth in our minds and our hearts.

Satan, Author of Lies and Deceit

To understand the amazing parallels between the Democrat party, Satan and his tactics we need to first understand how all of it began. How did Lucifer becomes Satan and why? Why is Satan bent on destroying the human race and causing is much evil suffering and death among us God's children.

Lucifer Becomes Satan…What Happened:

Theologians do not all agree on the details of what happened regarding Lucifer. There was a time in the universe where tranquility and perfection was enjoyed. Lucifer was referred to in biblical literature as "the anointed cherub". (Ezekiel 28:14) Lucifer was created as all the other angels were created.

Theologians do not all agree on what Lucifer did in heaven. In the book of Ezekiel it says , "you were the anointed cherub who covers, and I placed you there you were on the holy mountain of God ; you walked in the midst of the stones of fire " (v14) One interpretation is that he was in general service to the kingdom of God. Other theologians think the phrase refers to a priestly function associated with the cherubim. Lucifer may have directed and orchestrated the worship of other angels for God. No one knows for sure.

But then something terrible happened. Then, things took a turn for the worst in our universe because of what Lucifer did.

Your heart became proud on account of your beauty, and you corrupted your wisdom because of your splendor. So I threw you to the earth; I made a spectacle of you before kings. Ezekiel (28:17)

Unrighteousness was found within Lucifer. He fell in love with himself and then wanted to rule in heaven. He wanted dominion over all of creation, everything that God had created. This is how sin entered into our universe. It occurred within the spiritual realm. It occurred within the mind of Lucifer the morning star. He fell in love with only himself because of his great beauty.

> *You said in your heart, "I will ascend to the heavens; I will raise my throne above the stars of God; I will sit enthroned on the mount of assembly, on the utmost heights of Mount Zaphon I will ascend above the tops of the clouds; I will make myself like the Most High. Isaiah (14:13-14)*

This tragic decision by Lucifer brings up a fateful question that no one has been able to answer in thousands upon thousands of years. How can an unrighteous choice, out of the heart of a righteous being? How can that possibly happen if the potential for unrighteousness was not there? How can such an imperfection arise out of perfection? Nobody knows the answer to this. We will need to transcend our earthly limitations and brains before we understand the answer to this question. And for me, it is certain we will come to understand. So, what do we know about the current character, powers and limitations of Satan as he currently exists?

First, after his fall from God's grace Lucifer became known as Satan, the adversary, the opponent, the accuser (think all the Democrat accusations being made every day of our lives, it's the same thing. Democrats are the accusers of our time known as Satan). Job 1, Zechariah 3:1-2, 1 Chronicles 1:21. This name is from Hebrew.

What is the power of Satan?

> *For our struggle is not against flesh and blood, but against the rulers, against the powers, against the world forces of this darkness, against the spiritual forces of wickedness in the heavenly places. (Ephesians 6:12)*

Simply put Satan is not flesh and blood as we are. Rather he is a ruler of earth, the god of this earth that rules against Almighty God. Satan has the powers of this dark world aligned against the spiritual divine forces and against any and all Christians on planet earth. Our battle is not against flesh and blood, but against the evil one and all of his forces that inhabit the darkness.

Satan's Character, His Hatred, Evil Power, Destruction and Limitations: [11]

1. These forces CANNOT COMPEL anyone to sin against God. They are LIMITED! The children of God actually have power over Satan. We can simply say No to his lies, love God first and love our neighbors as we love ourselves. In my life I have had occasions to command demons out of the room. They obeyed in the name of Jesus Christ.
2. Satan is limited. He is not omnipresent omniscient and omnipotent. Satan does not have God like powers. Satan cannot be everywhere all the time. He is limited like you and me to one place at a time.
3. Satan is not all-knowing like God. He does not know everything, and he certainly does not understand everything.
4. Lastly, he is not all-powerful. He is very limited in what his powers are.
5. This is also true for all his demons.
6. Satan is not all-knowing like God. He does not know everything, and he certainly does not understand everything. Lucifer could not foresee or understand the consequences of any rebellion against God. When he and one third of the angels (Revelation 12:4) that followed him rebuild and were thrown out of heaven they must have been so very surprised.
7. Lastly, he is not all-powerful. He is very limited in what his powers are. He must rely on lies and deceit to manipulate people.
8. Satan does have free will just like all the rest of the Angels. He used his free will and chose to rebel against God. This legacy is what you and I are living in today.
9. After Satan's fall from heaven this became the situation:
   a. Satan was given the rulership of earth that would be allowed to spread his lies. (John 12: 31)
   b. God would give Satan time to see if he could rule his own kingdom successfully. Could he bring order out of the chaos that he created?
   c. God will not compromise his own holiness and justice. But he will meet Satan on earth winning a moral and spiritual victory over his enemy. God will win not just with power but by righteousness and love.
10. The battleground is inside of the human mind. The result of what happens inside our minds is displayed and become manifest for all the world to see in the physical realm through what we say and what we do.

---

[11] God's Devil, Irwin W. Lutzer, 2015, Moody Publishers

Satan Decides to Destroy the Human Race:

Satan came to hate God so much that his hate extended to anything God created. We are all children of God "made in His Image". Therefore, Satan hates us just as much as he hated Almighty God. He will do anything, say anything and lie and deceive anyone in order to bring about the destruction of God's children. You and I are in Satan's gun sights.

Based on the rhetoric that is constantly used by Democrat politicians it is clear to this writer that the radical liberals in the Democratic Party are using the very same tactic that Satan used to convince Adam and Eve to "eat the apple of the knowledge of good and evil". This was against the rules that God laid down for them. Because of this act of rebellion death now became inevitable for them, their children and all of their descendants in human history.

The garden of Eden was created for humankind. In it was ever so many delicious and healthy sources of food for Adam and Eve. There was only one tree that God expressly forbid them to eat from, the tree of the knowledge of good and evil. For both Adam and Eve knew that if they ate from that tree they would surely die. This is what God expressly told them. This tree was only one tree out of ever so many trees that populated the garden. Everything in the garden was wonderful beyond our contemporary imaginations.

Satan appeared to them as a snake. The snake must have been beautiful for Eve became very curious upon seeing it. Notice that Satan hid his real identity as the author of all lies and death. He disguised himself which in and of itself is a lie. Satan then told Eve that eating from the tree of the knowledge of good and evil would make them like God himself. Satan said you will surely not die. These are two of the biggest lies ever spoken in human history for believing these two lies all of human history and God's children has been altered permanently.

Satan took the one and only temptation laid before Adam and Eve and sold the idea to Adam and Eve that God was a liar. Satan said God lied to them when he told them that they would surely die if they ate from that single tree in the garden. He lied that they would become like God. He lied about his own appearance as a snake for surely if Satan appeared to them in his natural state, they would never believe a word that he said to them.

Satan had a hidden agenda. Satan lied about who he was. Satan lied about the tree of the knowledge of good and evil. Satan accused Almighty God of being the liar. So, you have the author of all lies, deceit, death and destruction lying about God being a liar. In the history of mankind after Adam and Eve, Satan has become the accuser that works against all of God's children. He accuses each of us of all our sins and argues that we should never be allowed into the kingdom of God, what we call heaven.

Satan in Everyday Life:

Since the fall of Satan and then Adam and Eve, evil has always been a plague against the human race. The constant battle between good and evil plays itself out inside our minds every day we live on planet earth. Everyone is affected. No one is immune.

Satan's Toolbox of Hate:

There are a multitude of ways that Satan uses to trick the human race and to motivate it to sin against God. There are however some common elements to the variety of tactics Satan uses to bring about the destruction of God's children. All of them have one common denominator, lies and deceit.

In the temptation and fall of Adam and Eve we see demonstrated some of the tactics Satan used against them. Satan displayed the workings of his evil mind.

1. Outright lies. As we saw above, Satan the author of all lies, lied to Adam and Eve that they would not die and instead they would become like God. Satan lied about who he was.
2. Accusations. Satan, the author of all lies and deceit, accused of God of being the liar when he told Adam and Eve if they ate of the tree of the knowledge of good and evil they would surely die.
3. Deceit
4. Hidden Agendas
5. Half Truths / Lies of Omission
6. Always angry about something and blaming other people
7. Never happy, never smiling or good natured,
8. Always negative in tone and content of what they say

The above are concrete signs of Satan occupying the minds of Democrats and other people as well. Don't need to be a Democrat to be a minion of Satan.

As Christians we all need to remember that it is, Satan the author of all lies, that came to deceive Adam and Eve accused God of deception. Satan is unable to speak truth therefore he accuses God of speaking untruth and lying. (The same thing Democrats are doing today against President Trump and other constitutional conservatives.) Satan always lies about himself and always tries to make himself look harmless and benevolent.

Then he spreads his lies to entrap people, lies about everything including God. Then he continues to make himself appear loving and innocent while he lies more and more about God.

Beware of people that accuse others. They are the real problem. Aka. Constant unending Democrat accusations Everything Democrats accuse President Trump of are exactly what they themselves are guilty of.

Original Sin, The False Bait:

In the case of Adam and Eve, the bait was the lie that they would become like Almighty God. It is human nature to always want something better. So too with the first couple. For every lie ever told, there needs to be some kind of bait. Becoming like God was the bait for Adam and Eve. Today we have a myriad of bait types.

For Democrats today they throw out lots of bait of different kinds. Consider this list:

1. Manmade CO2 is killing our planet. Life will be unsustainable. We will all die in 12 years. The Democrat Green New Deal will save the planet only if we act right now by electing Democrats to congress. They will be cosmic heroes saving us stupid people from ourselves. A great sense of urgency is added for further motivation to take the bait. NEVER trust someone that is selling something that there is a great urgency. NEVER!

2. Donald Trump colluded with the Russians to fix the 2016 election. He is an illegitimate president. All supporters of Donald Trump are also all of the above including deplorable

3. Racism, sexism, bigotry, homophobia, xenophobia, Islamophobia, misogyny, hatred and so many other hatreds exist in the United States.

4. White people are the problem in the United States. White supremacy is running rampant and is the source of much of the problems in the country.

5. Male toxicity is ruining our country. White males are a major problem. Never mind it is these people who created and developed our country, the best country in world history.

6. The constant drumbeat of character assassination against Trump or anyone who supports Trump. Here is a partial list of names: racist, bigot, liar in chief, Islamophobe, xenophobe, deplorable, irredeemable, greatest liar ever to sit in the white house, a sexist, demeaning, divisive, fascist,

Here are five example lies that we hear in the news every day we turn on the TV. All of this is courtesy of the radical left politicians that blather their mouths silly constantly selling the above lies to our public.

The Hook:

For every lie there must be something hidden from the victim of the lie. This is the hook. Once the hook becomes known, it is too late. Such is the nature of a hook. Ask any fish. In the five examples above, here are the hooks.

1. Objectively conducted science according to the scientific method has proven that mankind's role in global warming is miniscule. It has been shown time and time again that global warming as described by the Democrats is a hoax, just like the Russian collusion hoax they perpetrated on us for the last few years. A damned hoax of monster size and scope.

   We need to vote Democrat so we can save the planet. Democrats are the only ones that can save our earth from destruction. The hook is that the Green New Deal is an overwhelming monster socialist reform of every aspect of American life. This so called "deal" will create a socialist society where our current living standards will be destroyed for a complete false lie.

   This is 100% a complete lie. How do I know. The staff of Alexandria Ocasio Cortez said so. Saikat Chakrabarti, her chief of staff said this:

   "Do you guys think of it as a climate thing?" Because we really think of it as a how-do-you-change-the-entire-economy thing," Chakrabarti added. [12] NOT WHAT THEY SAID EARLIER. IT's CLIMATE CHANGE. The biggest hoax ever committed against our innocent population. I cannot right not think of a more

---

[12] https://dailycaller.com/2019/07/11/saikat-chakrabarti-green-new-deal/

monstrous lie ever told except when Satan told Adam and Eve they would be like God if they ate the fruit of the tree of the knowledge of good and evil.

The proposal also calls for "social, economic, racial, regional and gender-based justice and equality and cooperative and public ownership."

Note: Just think for a moment all the government regulation and personal surveillance requited to manage these socialist policies. The intrusion into our personal lives would be beyond what you can imagine today. However, the Chinese today in China are implementing just a technological system to monitor the behavior of every citizen with the help of OUR OWN HIGH TECH COMPANIES. How long before that same technology will be here. The Chinese people are being required to have a chip inserted to keep track of them to monitor them every second of their lives.

Christians call this "the mark of the beast". Woe to those who wear the mark of the beast!

Read that closely especially these last few words.

These are official code words for socialism and communism like "social justice". Mark this down very well. All this damned Green New Deal was NOT about the climate. They willfully, purposely LIED to all of us.

NO! Its about creating a new socialist/communist United States of America. They willfully lied to our entire country!! What kind of people does it take to create such monster lies? Satan possessed people, that is who.

The guise, the camouflage for this take over of our democratic republic is "climate change". This is the clown suit on Satan. They want to completely destroy the Judeo-Christian foundations that has brought so much success, wealth, health, well-being and high standards of living to the American People. It is assholes like the guy shown above that have this Satanic desire to destroy what we as a great nation have accomplished through blood, sweat and tears.

The Green New Deal will probably cost up to $93 trillion over a decade, according to a new report by the right-leaning American Action Forum (AAF). [13] but you are smart enough to know that government programs always overrun costs dramatically to the pain and agony of American citizens.

---

[13] https://dailycaller.com/2019/02/25/green-new-deal-cost-households/

Now, think about this. The guy you see above created this entire hoax called the Green New Deal claiming we all were going to die. Frankly, he looks like a skinny Che Guevarra. They specified completely socialist proposals to deal with the false problem that they emphasized was ever so true. This man knowingly lied to millions of Americans in an effort to move us to a socialist economy. That was the hook. Also notice his smile.

This guy is a revolutionary through and through. He is made of the same cloth as Fidel Castro, Che Guevarra and other socialist dictators. This Harvard-educated Saikat Chakrabarti is a huge fan of Indian political leader Subhas Chandra Bose who was an ally of Adolf Hitler and Imperial Japan during WWII. This educated idiot loves this fascist revolutionary so much that he wears a T-shirt with a picture of Subhas Chandra Bose on the front. Think of this people. We have Constantina Ocasio Cortez knowingly hiring a guy that idolizes an Indian fascist that fought with Adolph Hitler against the United States. Remember, this guy is a real fascist working for the Democrat party. What people don't know is that okay zero Cortez is also a hired actress and ex-barmaid. She is playing a theatrical part of Congresswoman and says and does what she is told to by people associated with a television program called "The Young Turks".

"You have to decide to create the society you want to create," he told Politico, "and that's done through politics." [14] **Notice how this bastard never once considers the needs and wants of "We the People".**

The scary thing is that there may be just enough ignorant Democrat voters to elect these kinds of liars into government where they can do lasting damage to our country. Our children are the ones who will pay the most for this lie. And notice this madman's smile.

The Punishment:

The punishment for us if we actually believe his lying Satanic tongue along with "The Squad", is we will experience pain, suffering and death because we believed this Satanic driven demon who looks human. Above is a picture of a demon in my opinion, taken over by Satan. Nobody else could even think of such awful lies to change a country with 325

---

[14] https://www.indiaabroad.com/indian-americans/saikat-chakrabarti-the-techie-behind-alexandria-ocasio-cortez/article_75240282-0187-11e9-a432-93f98a2205ce.html

million people in it. But, this is precisely what Satan has always wanted and targeted the United States for destruction.

Sadly, the punishment for Saikat Chakrabarti is probably nothing at all. He will be considered a hero by all those Satanic minions who have given over their brains and minds to the evil side of human nature. Always remember that Satan lives inside the minds of very many people to one degree or another. I personally cannot imagine what it takes to say such horrific lies that would cause so much pain, agony suffering and death to our entire nation. Chakrabarti knows though for this is exactly what this monster has done.

The False Bait:

the entire Democrat political platform as outlined in another part of this literary work is the false bait being offered to the American people. Look at precisely what they want to do and ask yourself what is it going to take to do this. Ask yourself how much more government is needed to implement all of this. Ask yourself how many more days in the year of my productive life will I have to have confiscated from me by the government. It is a Satan -sized monster that will be put on your back every day you still live on this planet Earth.

The latest big lie is that Donald Trump colluded with the Russians to alter the 2016 election resulting with him winning the presidency. Therefore, he is an illegitimate president and should be immediately impeached. The false proof is a dossier written by British spy Christopher Steele. We must remove Trump so as to preserve the integrity of our federal government.

Has anyone in this country ever noticed that during the last few years there was never any evidence presented to us the American people that Donald Trump colluded with the Russians? No evidence was ever directly presented, none. Yet, for two years every day we heard from the Democrat party and the propaganda outlets of CNN, MSNBC and CBS and so many other paid for liberal lying machines that Trump was guilty as sin and must be impeached.

Now, after the putrid Mueller report has been released, we find out that Mueller did not write the damned report that bears his name. In his last testimony before Congress Mueller could not answer simple questions about his own report. He showed complete unfamiliarity with its contents. Now we do not know who really wrote the report, other than to say there were 18 rabid Democrat Trump haters and Hillary Clinton donors appointed as his staff to investigate the report. Answer to yourself truthfully this question, do you believe 18 Democrat Hillary Clinton donors will remain unbiased against Donald Trump in their investigation? If you do, please send me $1 million.

Another false accusation against Pres. Trump tied to real corruption by Joe and Hunter Biden: [15]

The most recent lie as of September 2019 is that during a normal governmental conversation with the president of the Ukraine, the Democrats are now accusing Pres. Trump of putting "undue pressure" on the Ukrainian president to investigate the already documented corruption by Joe Biden trying to cover for his corrupt son named Hunter Biden. It seems Hunter manipulated a multibillion-dollar deal where he wound up with many millions of unearned dollars for political favors granted to you the Ukrainians by the Obama administration. All this is well documented on like the Russian collusion hoax. I have seen videos of Joe Biden bragging about his threat to Ukraine that if they did not cease the investigation into his son for corruption, he would make sure they did not get hit $1 billion loan guarantee. This is corruption of the highest and worst kind. Joe Biden is certainly guilty of it and the videos that are in the public domain prove it.

Russian Collusion and The Hook:

The dossier was bought and paid for by the Hillary Clinton campaign as an insurance policy that if somehow Trump won the election, they can claim he cheated with the Russians and will be removed from office.

Ten Other Signs That Say Democrats Have Strong Satanic Influences in Them:

1. Attempted assassination of Republican Steve Scalise at a practice congressional baseball game by James Hodgkinson a Bernie Sanders supporter.

2. Tim Kaine calls on liberals to "fight in the streets" against Trump supporters. [16] This is a call for violence against Trump supporters.

3. "Shakespeare in the Park" in New York depicts the assassination of Donald Trump. [17]

15
https://duckduckgo.com/?q=video+joe+biden+Ukraine+billion+dollar+deal+&t=chromentp&atb=v168-1&iax=videos&ia=videos&iai=KCF9My1vBP4
[16] https://youtu.be/GWvqn8F7YMs
[17] https://youtu.be/vFOxpcpiNzo

4. Obama-appointed Attorney General Loretta Lynch calls for liberals to march, bleed and die in the streets as they "resist" Trump. [18]

5. Madonna publicly wishes and thinks about blowing up the White House at a Women's march in Washington D.C.

6. New Snoop Dogg music video features the rapper executing a clown-faced Trump. [19]

7. Barack Obama encouraged people to "argue with them and get in their face", talking about Trump supporters. [20]

8. Who can forget poor little Kathy Griffin and her blood soaked head of a decapitated Donald Trump? She blames president Trump for all her self inflicted wounds.

9. The "Blame Game" was in full swing after Hillary lost the election. People inspired by Satan never take responsibility for their own actions.

10. Keith Olbermann insisted that Vladimir Putin put Trump in power and is now his puppet.

11. The long history of the Democrat party being the party of slavery, yes slavery including support for the KKK and so many horrific actions against black people over many years.

12. The immigration "concentration camp" hoax perpetrated by Alexandria Ocasio Cortez posing as if at a detention center for children, crying for them. The picture on the right is what people were supposed to see. A distraught crying

13. AOC for all the mistreated children by that awful Donald Trump. There are two problems with this LIE. The truth is that she posed for this publicity stunt in front of a chain link fence parking lot. You can see the police car in the background. The second truth is that it is Barack Obama that instituted this separation of children from adults because a very large percentage of kids were NOT the children of the adult they were with. This is called child trafficking, a felony with jail time. But it was OK for Obama to do this but NOT that

---

[18] https://youtu.be/tEHJKJLp1g8
[19] https://youtu.be/zIkriVtLMdA
[20] https://youtu.be/N1AOePp4r98

miserable terrible Donald Trump. The picture on the left is the truth of where AOC was performing her sobbing act.

On top of all this arranged fake drama by Democrats we find in the news the following:

Headline:

Nearly 6,000 Fake Families Found at Border, Illegals Released into U.S. Within 48 Hours. [21]

The Border Patrol has apprehended nearly 6,000 fake families at the southwest border, and now devotes upwards of 60 percent of its manpower in high-crossing areas on what amounts to babysitting. Even worse, the agency is releasing so-called families into the interior with virtually no vetting.

Satan must have been proud of this effort to lie to the American people. Question: how can anyone believe anything AOC or her "Squad" says after knowing about this immigration lying hoax and the Green New Deal intended to totally destroy the economy of the United States under the lie of "climate change". I can only believe that Satan is the force behind the complete dishonesty, lies and deceit perpetrated by the Democrat Party directly against the health and well being of the American people.

What kind of monster willfully and purposely lies such big lies against the people of our country? They look like human beings but the deeper I dig into the truth of things the more retched the stench becomes. Remember, it is a mark of Satan to lust for power and dominion over God's children. The Christian heart seeks to serve the best interest of other people in our spiritual journey to Almighty God. It is the lust for power and control that burn inside the heart of Satan and the Democrats of today.

All the above items show a complete breakdown of civility and respect for other human beings all because Democrats are disagreed with. I have yet to see any Democrat on TV give a fact based reason for a political position that is not somehow twisted or

---

[21] https://www.blabber.buzz/conservative-news/628171-nearly-6000-fake-families-found-at-border-illegals-released-into-us-within-48-hours-special?utm_source=c-mid&utm_medium=c-mid-email&utm_term=c-mid-Yahoo

mutated by scatterbrain thinking. The above ten examples are just the tip of the iceberg. Space does not allow more but there is indeed much more.

A Working Definition of Evil:

Evil is any non-loving action taken against a child of God that purposely intends to damage that person from doing what they are supposed to do while here on earth. In other words, anything that interferes with the working out of God's plan for each of His children, destroys order, produces or leads to chaos, suffering and pain.

Evil by its nature must be founded upon lies of either commission or omission or half-truths intended to deceive and manipulate people into doing unholy things. Evil always seeks **dominion** over others of God's children. An evil person always appears different to others than they really are. They must always put on a mask to hide their true identity.

Evil normally occurs in the physical realm. However, nothing happens in the physical realm that has not occurred in our minds first. The idea of evil thoughts is valid and precedes acting out these evil thoughts with evil actions. The source of evil, supernatural and psychological is in our minds where the war between good and evil exists. Our minds are the battlefield of God verses Satan. This is part of our nature as human beings ever since the fatal choice of Eve and then Adam to seek the "knowledge of good and evil".

Every one of God's children has personal boundaries. These boundaries are to be respected by all people. These boundaries include, physical, moral, mental, emotional and includes all the necessary space around a child of God. Evil by its very nature violates personal boundaries and codes of loving morality as its intent is to destroy all sanctity of a person. Dishonoring a person's boundaries is an act of evil.

Evil by its nature has its source in the spiritual realm, it enters the minds of people and is fought off by a child of God preventing evil to manifest its damage in the physical realm. Evil wishes to destroy loving order in order to produce chaos, suffering and pain.

Evil and Good has roots within the spiritual realm. Good and evil are not two sides of the same coin. They are not binary concepts. Shades of grey where absence of one does not imply the existence of the other. Evil would not be noticeable to us were it not for all the good in the world.

Satan and The Democrat Party:

Most people think that the political problems the United States has today is somehow new and unique and different from things before. Nothing could be further from the truth. The United States of America has always been a target for Satan to destroy. If you look at the rest of the world you will find that it is mired in very serious problems. People have far lower living standards than we do in America. People have much less freedom in so many different ways than we do here also. I have traveled the world in my business career and I have to tell you that if you live in the United States of America you are very lucky indeed. Never ever believe the gutter sludge that is spewed out the mouths of Democrats when they trash this Judeo-Christian country. These Democrats are willfully and purposely doing the bidding of Satan and his lost and hate for God to destroy this Judeo-Christian country.

These problems stem from countries like Russia, United States, or ran, North Korea, Japan, Germany, China and other large powerful countries all trying to outdo each other both economically and militarily. In other words, everybody wants to be top dog. This simply means that everybody wants domination over everybody else. This is why every new technology that has ever been invented is always, and I mean always, been used first as a weapon of war. Of course, we call this increasing our capability for defense and security.

The lust for dominion is the root of all evil in this world. This inherent desire and lust that is in the minds of every human being is demonstrated anywhere from the elementary school yard all the way through to the highest positions of power in state governments across the world.

This is the condition of mankind. There is a war that continues to rage in the minds of every human being. And as was pointed out earlier it all started when Lucifer fell in love with himself because of his beauty that God had created him to be. He then decided to put his throne higher than God. He was thrown out of the heavenly kingdom, became Satan the adversary and the hater of anything made in the image of God. This is you and me.

Satan is an evil spirit and has the abilities to influence people that are so inclined to do evil. As this is written there is a huge war going on for the body and soul of the United States government.

It matters not what people think but the truth is our country, the United States of America was founded by white European men and women who came here with firm beliefs and Christianity. These Christian beliefs and principles of conduct and rules for government are the fundamental and foundational reason why the United States has been the greatest country ever devised by mankind. It is because our founding fathers and so many others that came here from Europe had Christianity in their hearts. They obeyed both of God's top two commandments. The first is to love God with all your mind with all your heart and all your soul above all else. The second is like the first, love your neighbor as you love yourself.

There were different denominations of Christianity in the early days of the United States. These different denominations got along with each other because the unifying factor in their lives was Almighty God himself.

No one in their right mind, no one who is the slightest bit honest will ever deny the fact that the United States of America was founded on Judeo-Christian principles by white European men and women who came here so long ago. Were it not for these immigrants into this country the contiguous 48 states would remain a wilderness and things like mankind reaching the moon would never have happened.

Our world however is in very bad shape. There is such turmoil, hatred, war, tyranny, diseases and sicknesses that are spreading across the world today. Now we have illegal immigrants coming to the United States and they bring with them diseases that they were never vaccinated against. As of today, as this is written there is now many episodes of typhoid in Los Angeles. Measles, once eradicated from this country, is now making a comeback in sanctuary cities.

Make no mistake about it, the United States is very much in the crosshairs of Satan as he wants nothing less than the total destruction of this Christian country. We hear all the time that all the religions are equal. This is a Satanic lie. I repeat, this is a Satanic lie. To understand this lie all one has to do is to look around the world at where all the religions are prominent. You will find great suffering pain and death in the countries that are Buddhist, Hindu, Muslim and others.

The Judeo-Christian beliefs, principles and foundational loving elements for a working society is what has propel the United States to the great heights that we have achieved as a country. Are we perfect? No. Nothing that mankind is involved with can ever be perfect simply because of the war that continues to rage on inside everyone's head between evil attacking the good.

Government by its very nature has such evil associated with it including here in the United States. It is evil for any government to confiscate 40% of the productive life of one of God's children. These monies are taken and confiscated through our tax policy enforced by a tremendous amount of weaponry that can be aimed at the taxpayer. God said that 10% was enough but our government especially the Democrats will want eventually everything that you have and earn. This is so they may pay off voters to vote for them and they can remain in power over the rest of us. Our government no longer views itself as the people's servant. It views itself as the only legitimate authority that deserves eternal life and domination over every US citizen.

Remember this always: Satan works through the minds of human beings. He is clever and stealthy and always a fisherman of men's souls. He throws out the bait that contains a deadly hook to snare those gullible enough and misguided or weak enough to take the bait. Then Satan has you. This is precisely what has been happening in the United States of America for the past 50 to 60 years. To this writer it all started with Madeleine Murray O'Hare, the atheist who attacked God at every turn in our public life. I saw her on TV many times. She was a nasty woman frankly and ended up being murdered because of her dealings with other people.

Now we see the Democrats en masse promoting the very things that Satan wants them to promote. The Democrats of today were described back in 1965 by Paul Harvey a highly respected commentator of the time. Below is Paul's warning to all of us. He was warning us of Satan, Satan's tactics and his strategy to destroy the United States of America.

Read his warning below and stop and think, and I mean really think about what he said back in 1965 and how those very things are manifesting in occurring today within the policies, the platform and the rhetoric of the presidential candidates of the Democrat party. Everything the Democrats are proposing today are exactly what Satan wants them to do and what Paul Harvey warned us about 55 years ago.

You see, there's really nothing new under the sun. Evil from Satan simply uses different people under different circumstances saying different things that all amount of the same thing. It is going against God's will and his love for all of us. The 2020 election is probably going to be one of the biggest turning points in the history of the United States. We are in danger of going off the Democrat party socialist Cliff that will result in the United States being nothing more than a Cuba, a Venezuela, a China or a Russia all of which are really Third World countries with militaries of various sizes.

After reading this if anybody votes for a single Democrat in the 2020 election I can only say that you to have been infected by Satan in your mind and you have no excuse when your time comes to explain your life to God.

If I Were Satan: [22]

Paul Harvey was one of the most famous radio personalities of the 20th century. He first went on the air in 1933, and with shows like The Rest of the Story he was a staple of

---

[22] https://churchpop.com/2017/07/05/paul-harveys-startling-prescient-devil-speech/

America radio for decades. He was also a devout Christian who was deeply concerned that the United States was abandoning God and morality at her own peril. The below essay was written in the 1960's when conditions in the United States were much better than they are now. We had problems to be sure, but our country was far more united, and the Democrat party was not the Satanic version of itself that it has grown into today.

Remember what I have said before. The United States is the last and only country that has been created under the Judeo-Christian principles and values that Almighty God ordained for all of mankind. This is the reason that we are the best country to live in today. But we are under vicious attack from all quarters and from within by the Democrat party, the party of Satan himself. We in this country are this planet's only hope of spiritual survival. This thought is ever so important. If we lose the United States to Satan as the Democrats are hell bent on doing, the entire world will fall to Satan. Of this there is no doubt.

We are fighting a spiritual war against Satan who is sometimes called the Prince of Darkness. This battle or war is being conducted inside the minds of every human being, every American citizen. Our weapons against evil is simply the objective truth of things. Remember that Jesus Christ is "the way, the truth and the life", no one goes to Almighty God the Father except through Him.

The weapons Satan uses are a myriad of lies, deceit, falsehoods and other devious plans in order to deceive and trick people into doing sinful damaging and destructive things against others and themselves. Avoid any person that disregards God or attacks God's commandments and His churches. Also avoid people who do unto others that they do not want done to themselves. These are the signs of people destined to hell.

Remember also that I have personally had multiple direct and hate filled episodes with this hateful beast and a few of his demons. Do not despair though. We have power over Satan and all the darkness from his demons. Simply do what I have done. Command them to leave you, tell them go back to hell where you belong in the name of Jesus Christ. This has worked for me every time. I am on Satan's shit list but know how to protect myself along with the divine protection that I know I have.

Remember this again: Satan is indeed very real along with his demons. You too have power over this darkness as a child of God. Command them to vanish in the name of Jesus Christ. This is all you need to do. They will flee. One last additional thought. Satanic demons are very afraid of Mother Mary, the sinless divine human being who gave birth to Jesus Christ. Her purity is something anyone associated with Satan cannot stand to be near.

The following was written by Paul Harvey, a wonderful wise man who was a devoted Christian and should be listened to by anyone who has any faith at all. You do not need to be a committed Christian in order to benefit from Paul's great thoughts about our country.

Published in 1964:

If I were the prince of darkness, I would want to engulf the whole world in darkness.

I'd have a third of its real estate and four-fifths of its population, but I would not be happy until I had seized the ripest apple on the tree — thee.

So, I would set about however necessary to take over the United States.

I'd subvert the churches first, and I would begin with a campaign of whispers.

With the wisdom of a serpent, I would whisper to you as I whispered to Eve: "Do as you please."

To the young, I would whisper that the Bible is a myth. I would convince the children that man created God instead of the other way around. I'd confide that what's bad is good and what's good is square.

And the old, I would teach to pray after me, "Our Father, which are in Washington ..."

Then, I'd get organized, I'd educate authors in how to make lurid literature exciting so that anything else would appear dull and uninteresting.

I'd peddle narcotics to whom I could. I'd sell alcohol to ladies and gentlemen of distinction. I'd tranquilize the rest with pills.

If I were the devil, I'd soon have families at war with themselves, churches at war with themselves and nations at war with themselves until each, in its turn, was consumed.

And with promises of higher ratings, I'd have mesmerizing media fanning the flames.

If I were the devil, I would encourage schools to refine young intellect but neglect to discipline emotions. I'd tell teachers to let those students run wild. And before you knew it, you'd have drug-sniffing dogs and metal detectors at every schoolhouse door.

With a decade, I'd have prisons overflowing and judges promoting pornography. Soon, I would evict God from the courthouse and the schoolhouse and them from the houses of Congress.

In his own churches, I would substitute psychology for religion and deify science. I'd lure priests and pastors into misusing boys and girls and church money.

If I were the devil, I'd take from those who have and give to those who wanted until I had killed the incentive of the ambitious.

What'll you bet I couldn't get whole states to promote gambling as the way to get rich?

I'd convince the young that marriage is old-fashioned, that swinging is more fun and that what you see on television is the way to be.

And thus, I could undress you in public and lure you into bed with diseases for which there are no cures.

In other words, if I were the devil, I'd just keep right on doing what he's doing.

Commentary:

The subversion of the Churches is intense. Muslims kill Christian every day of the week all over the world. I donate substantial money to the Iraqi Christian Relief fund to help those poor people recover from what ISIS has done to them. After ISIS is forced to move out of an area, it looks like an atomic bomb went off. Nothing is left standing as their goal is to kill, kill and kill again while destroying anything that can be used by refugees that return to their former homes.

So many priests and other clergy have been seduced by Satan into being child abusers and sex abusers. Far more today then when Paul wrote his essay above.

Satan said, "Do as you please". These are the exact words Democrat mayor of New York and Democrat presidential candidate Bill De Blasio said on the 2020 campaign trail to young people. He went on to say, come to New York and be whatever you want to be and do your own thing. For your truth is your own different from the rest. We in government will have your back. In other words, there is no objective morality. Morality is different for each person. BULLSHOOT! There are two great commandments. Love God above all else with all your heart, your mind and your soul. The second great commandment is to love all your neighbors as you love yourself. It is really simple actually. Remember this.

Teach all the kids that the Bible is a false myth. There is no God really. The idea of God is something that man has created. BULLSHOOT! I have personally been to heaven dear reader. It is my solemn testimony to you that heaven exists no matter what you choose to believe. One day you will indeed see for yourself. Democrats are anti-Christian and attack Christians who are nominated for high political office in government. I do not know if I will be able to look down far enough to see the likes of Diane Feinstein, Maxine Waters, Barack Obama and all the others of Satan's minions after my time is finished on this perverted earth. The children of Almighty God will never have to deal with these perverted creatures again in all eternity. Thank you Lord.

Democrat's god is central government which they want to control on an absolute basis. This is why Paul said, "Our father which art in Washington." Washington DC is actually a hellhole. There are more sociopaths and psychopaths in DC than in any other place in the United States. Why? Because political power attracts these people like turds attract flies and other insects. Remember what mayor Marion Barry said a few years ago. "Gee, if you don't count all the murders in Washington DC, our crime rate isn't all that high." Pathetic!

We have Hollywood promoting vicious killing as a form of entertainment. **I would tax hollywood and others in the entertainment industry for every depiction of killing and death as a form of entertainment.** This just twists and mutates the minds of our young to be ambivalent to violence in real life. Any of the so called polls that say different are just like the so called climate change investigations that are proven to be false. We have Democrats who actively fight all attempts to get rid of illegal and lethal drugs coming into our country from Mexico and other places. This is exactly what Satan wants his minion Democrats to do for him in order to destroy this country.

Satan would have Almighty God evicted from all public places, schools and other places that are visible to "We the People". Back in the 1960's there were far more expressions of our Judeo-Christian heroes to be seen when you travel around the country. Madalyn Murry O'Hare the atheist let a concentrated effort to have God removed from all public places. She did this right up until the time she was murdered by another atheist of her group. Today we remove anything that is a Godly statue, or anything that reminds us of God or even our Judeo-Christian roots as a nation because Democrats say it "might offend someone". Well, BULLSHOOTY on that. We are a Christian nation and how can any loving person want to exterminate signs of our faith and our history. Democrats do, that is who. This is exactly what Satan wants and the Democrats are willfully doing his will.

Satan wants to take from those who work hard and give the money to those who do not want to in the name of fairness. This removes all incentives to work hard for your future and rewards those who sit on their asses. So, you get far more ass sitting as a result with all the excuses in the world why people sit so much and watch perverted TV shows that talk about psychology and how unfair life is. Boo Hoo Hoo!

Satan wants to destroy the institution of marriage between man and woman. Democrats have been attacking the sacrament of marriage for a long time now. Like it or not, God's creation, this universe, has two genders only. Yes some people are born somehow with an attraction to the same gender they are. These people are to be loved as any other of God's children. We are NOT to judge but love them as ourselves. It is just that simple. But today, the Democrat party promotes gender confusion through different methods. They claim male toxicity, so they want to make boys into girls. They claim that there are no binary genders. Rather each person falls somewhere in between the two genders. Everyone is a mix of male and female. BULLSHOOTY! But they want this gender distinction to be destroyed. This is evil right at its heart so people will not know how to relate to each other. They want to create a muddy mess and are having some success at this Satanic gambit.

Finally, after reading all this, it should be obvious that the Democrat party and its policies should be viewed only as a Satanic branch of hell on earth.

The Ugly Hateful History of the Democrat Party:

The accurate history of the Democrat party is not a pleasant thing to read about. It is full of the very things they accuse conservatives and other people of. Things like racism, homophobia, bigotry and other ugly human behavior sponsored by Satan.

Everything you are about to read is true history of the Democrat party. I encourage everyone to do your own research on this topic. Objective history will confirm what is presented here.

*"The Democratic Party is the oldest voter-based political party in the world and the oldest existing political party in the United States, tracing its heritage back to the anti-Federalists and the Jeffersonian Democratic-Republican Party of the 1790s.[1][2][3] Known as the party of the "common man", the early Democratic Party stood for individual rights and state sovereignty and **opposed banks and the abolition of slavery.**"* [23]

Headline: An 1872 print by Currier and Ives depicts the first seven black Americans elected to the U.S. Congress during the Reconstruction period of 1865 to 1877-- and they're all Republican! [24] Clearly, the true history of the Democrat party is quite opposite of what almost all people think it is. People thing Democrats protected blacks. NO! It is the opposite. Democrats opposed ending slavery.

Clearly, the latter half of the 19th Century, and for much of the early half of the 20th Century, it was the Republican Party that was the party of choice for blacks. How can this be? Because the Republican Party was formed in the late 1850s as an oppositional force to the pro-slavery Democratic Party.

---

[23] https://en.wikipedia.org/wiki/History_of_the_United_States_Democratic_Party

[24]

https://www.americanthinker.com/articles/2016/05/the_secret_racist_history_of_the_democratic_part y.html

Republicans wanted to return to the principles that were originally established in the republic's founding documents and in doing so became the first party to openly advocated strong civil rights legislation. Voters took notice and in 1860 Abraham Lincoln was elected President along with a Republican Congress. This infuriated the southern Democrats, who soon afterwards left Congress and took their states with them to form what officially became known as The Slaveholding Confederate States of America. [25]

This last part shows the seeds being sown for the civil war. Southern Democrats loved having slaves and would fight to the death to keep them. When I was a little boy visiting family in Petersburg Virginia, I still remember the language they used against blacks and the vocabulary they used as well. Simply put, the were racists.

Democrats were against the abolition of slavery as well. These days they do everything they can to hide this historical fact. Here is the truth of things:

a. The 13th amendment to the constitution officially abolished slavery in 1864. Here is the voting record.

   a. Democrats for 19.   Democrats against 82
   b. Republicans for 118   Republicans against ZERO

   From this we can see just how racist the democrat party was. It still is believe it or not.

b. The 14th and 15th amendments guaranteeing the rights of citizenship and voting rights to blacks. Here are the voting results.

   a. Democrats for ZERO   Democrats against 101
   b. Republicans for 118   Republicans against ZERO

These votes were to make it the law that all blacks should be full-fledged citizens of the United States of America. I find it completely remarkable that people today do not know this tawdry miserable history of the Democrats. Not only this but it gets **worse**! Most of our Southern states have been initially formed and or heavily influenced by the black community as members of the Republican party, not the dishonest lying Democrat party.

25

https://www.americanthinker.com/articles/2016/05/the_secret_racist_history_of_the_democratic_party.html

Democrats completely opposed blacks becoming citizens and having all basic human rights. It became law because of Republicans!

Source: American Thinker: [26]

*"In spite of this, in almost every Southern state, **the Republican Party was actually formed by blacks, not whites.** Case in point is Houston, Texas, where 150 blacks and 20 whites created the Republican Party of Texas. But perhaps most telling of all with respect to the Republican Party's achievements is that black men were continuously elected to public office. For example, 42 blacks were elected to the Texas legislature, 112 in Mississippi, 190 in South Carolina, 95 representatives and 32 senators in Louisiana, and many more elected in other states -- all Republican. Democrats didn't elect their first black American to the U.S. House until 1935!"*

Just stop for a moment and think about the preceding paragraph. All along you have been propagandized that Democrats are the party of civil rights protection. NO! They were the party in favor of slavery and organized to keep the black community down.

KKK Emblem in 1860's

Just think of this. Racism seems to always be front and center in the minds of Democrats. It is in their DNA. Race has been a very important topic on the minds of ever so many Democrats throughout our history as a nation. Because, the facts shown above is only part of the story. It gets even more worse. Proceeding onward through history with the Democrat party and their attitudes toward black people we get into the mid 1860's.

26

https://www.americanthinker.com/articles/2016/05/the_secret_racist_history_of_the_democratic_party.html

One of the most vivid examples of collusion between the KKK and Democratic Party was when Democrat Senator Wade Hampton ran for the governorship of South Carolina in 1876. The Klan put into action a battle plan to help Democrats win, stating: "Every Democrat must feel honor bound to control the vote of at least one Negro by intimidation…. Democrats must go in as large numbers…and well-armed." An issue of Harper's Weekly that same year illustrated this mindset with a depiction of two white Democrats standing next to a black man while pointing a gun at him. At the bottom of the depiction is a caption that reads: "Of Course He Wants To Vote The Democratic Ticket!" [27]

There were also lynchings, but not what you might think. According to the University of Missouri-Kansas City School of Law, between 1882 and 1964 an estimated 3,446 blacks and 1,279 whites were lynched at the hands of the Klan. Why? FOR THE VERY SAME REASON DEMOCRATS TALK ABOUT TODAY, POLITICALLY INCORRECT SPEECH. If you disagree with Democrats, that makes you a criminal in their eyes. It was true back in the 18th century and it is true today! See, you think that this politically correct speech is something new along with the book by George Orwell, 1984. NOPE! Democrats have been pumping this bilge for hundreds of years. They have been dropping it in public for as long too.

KKK Flag in 1860's

Turds of Democrat Wisdom Just Keep Coming

The fundamental goal of the KKK was to use violence and other tactics against Republicans who were fighting for full civil rights of the black community. Yes, it was Democrats that were underneath those white KKK pointed head dresses. This truth is much different than what you have been probably taught in school. Well, school is another terrible topic of truth. You have been lied to by both lies of commission and lies

---

[27]

https://www.americanthinker.com/articles/2016/05/the_secret_racist_history_of_the_democratic_party.html

of omission. When it comes to history you have been lied to by lies of omission. School systems just ignore the inconvenient facts of the Democrat Party history.

In South Carolina, for example, the Klan even passed out "push cards" -- a hit list of 63 (50 blacks and 13 whites) "Radicals" of the legislature pictured on one side and their names listed on the other. Democrats called Republicans radicals not just because they were a powerful political force, but because they allowed blacks to participate in the political process. Apparently, this was all too much for Democrats to bear. [28]

---

[28] IBID

Examples of hate speech from Democrats

Al Sharpton:

"White folks was in caves while we was building empires… We taught philosophy and astrology and mathematics before Socrates and them Greek Homo's ever got around to it."
Al Sharpton, 1994 speech at Kean College, New Jersey

There are white n*ggers. I've seen a lot of white n*ggers in my time. [29] Al Sharpton

While the rest of the country waves the flag of Americana, we understand we are not part of that. We don't owe America anything - America owes us. [30] Al Sharpton

I don't know the difference between the words was and were. So, I'll just stick to racism against whites. I like that better. Al Sharpton

Notice how Al thinks that white America owes Blacks. Notice how he drives a racial wedge between the black community and the rest of the United States. This is precisely how Satan works. He finds differences between people and then claims one group is taking advantage of another group. This talk breeds racial hatred. Al Sharpton is one of the worst racists we have in the country today. He is the Sen. Byrd of the black community. Funny thing is, they are both hateful Democrats. There are many more racist quotes from my sources. I used three because I got sick of it. Jesus Christ has said there are two great commandments. First is to love God first and above all else. The second commandment is like the first. You are to love your neighbor as you love yourself. Satan on the other hand is the author of all lies and deceit. Which one of these two do you think Al Sharpton is listening to? Which one of these two, God or Satan does Al Sharpton have in his heart of hearts? This is one disgusting and wretched man. Anybody who listens to one word from this racist monster is a complete blithering idiot.

---

[29] https://www.azquotes.com/quote/727020
[30] IBID

Hillary Clinton:

"You ***king Jew bastard" said to Paul Fray, a political operative. Jerry Oppenheimer, said: "Three witnesses have now publicly acknowledged that she said it."

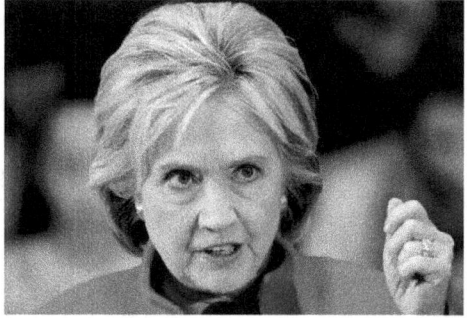

As First Lady, Hillary called young black men *"super-predators"* indicating that she thought all young black males were violent criminals. She also said, *"We have to bring them to heel,"* [31]

Grandma Clinton admires Margaret Sanger very much. Margaret is the founder of Planned Parenthood. She was a complete racist and birth control activist.

"I admire Margaret's anger enormously, her courage her tenacity her vision..." Hillary Clinton

One quote from Margaret who Hillary worships so much:

"Colored people are like human weeds and need to be exterminated." Margaret Sanger

In other articles and resources that I have researched I have found that the reason Margaret Sanger wanted aggressive birth control was to get rid of Blacks in our country. Apparently, Hillary Clinton likes this idea a lot to her admiration of Sanger. And the Democrat party was so much in love with Hillary Clinton they nominated her to run for president in 2016. What does this tell you about the Democrat party in general regarding their true feelings about racism and other topics? It does not take much thinking to figure this out.

---

[31] https://downtrend.com/71superb/top-ten-examples-of-hillary-clintons-racism-the-media-chooses-to-ignore/

Elizabeth Warren:

This woman perpetrated a fraud on Harvard University. On her application she specified that she was part native American Indian. It is completely untrue. It has been proven completely untrue through DNA testing. Now, by applying the Democrat party's own criteria for judging people, this makes Elizabeth Warren guilty of fraud, guilty of racial appropriation and guilty of cultural appropriation of the American Indians. She is guilty all over the place and she lectures people in her speeches on how moral they are supposed to be according to liberal ethics. BULLSHOOTY!

I ask what kind of person does it take to lie about their own lily white skin color with blonde hair and disown her own racial features and lie about being something else instead. It takes a terribly dishonest person with no morals or standards of Christian conduct whatsoever.

If you are a Democrat, you just gotta have "reservations" about voting for this female creature. Get it?

Because of her fraud to the University she has a professorship that pays $350,000 per year that gives her enough time to run for president of the United States. How nice, how cushy how wonderful for this dishonest woman.

Her Awful Socialist Policies:

Warren's expressed socialist policies she wants to force down our throats is an effective way to destroy the economy of the United States. **The premise and reasons she states to justify these policies are all completely FALSE.**

She completely bashes who she calls the rich. Who is the "rich"? Warren never states a criteria. This is a snake in the grass Satanic tactic to generate hate toward other people who may have more wealth than others. She is willfully, purposely and with animus toward successful people sowing seeds of hatred against those people who worked their asses off, saved their money and managed their lives in a successful way. For this Pocahontas wants everyone to hate them for that. This violates the second great commandment which is to love your neighbor as you love yourself. Warren does the exact opposite and wants people to hate each other based on crazy perceptions of who has more money. From this alone, it is honest and forthright to label this socialist creature as a minion of Satan doing his work here on planet earth.

She hates completely the economic system, free market capitalism, that has produced all the wealth in this country which has in turn made the United States the best country in the world to live in and the best country ever created by mankind. I say again, our country's economic system and social policies are founded upon Judeo-Christian principles and ethics. Remember the following rules for a successful life.

The closer you are to the two great commandments, the far better life you will have regarding health, well-being, wealth and being a loving positive influence to all of God's children. These two great commandments are very simple.

1.   Love Almighty God first above all else with all your mind, your heart and soul
2.   Love your neighbor as you love yourself

Elizabeth Warren is so far away from these foundational principles that you would need a high power telescope to find her. Frankly, she is sowing the seeds of her own destruction in eternity. In this I pray for her and pity her at the same time.

In bashing our free market capital economic system, she is also attacking the very Judeo-Christian principles that has made this country is great as it is producing all the freedoms that you enjoy today. If she gets elected I guarantee you this country will start a painful slide into the hell hole known as socialism.

In light of the well-known facts leading socialism and its documented 100% failure rate in world history how can this woman possibly entertained such an idea that is so consistent with the destruction of God's children so very much wanted by Satan himself. She wants to bring destruction to our country and to our people. This is precisely what Satan wants as well. Therefore, I can only conclude that this woman has for her own personal reasons, she has become a minion of Satan, consciously, willfully and purposely. Her lust for dominion and political power supersedes everything else including the health and well-being of all the American people.

If anybody votes for this satanically inspired woman, you're out of your stinking mind.

Here are some of the details, the ugly details of what she wants to do to us if given political power:

1. she hates wealthy people. She wants to implement a wealth tax. Simply put what this means is whatever your investments are above a certain level the government will take something like two or 3% of your total wealth away from you. They will confiscate a portion of your wealth every year. If you are wealth and stocks and bonds goes up by 4% in one year the government will tax the 4% but then also confiscate an additional two or 3% from your starting balance.

    If you had $100,000 in your stock account and you gained $4000 in profit, the government will take about 40% of that or $2400 in gains tax. Pocahontas then through the wealth tax will take between $2000 and $3000 of the original $100,000 starting balance. This leaves you with not a $4000 gain but a $600 loss for the year. Without these amounts of money that we call capital there will be no money to spend on important projects to maintain and increase the health and well-being of our country. This is the huge problem in Third World countries, precisely this. She wants to murder the engine of our economic prosperity through the false notion of fairness, her brand of fairness which is to tear down the wealth that has been created by the producers and workers in our country.

    This single idea goes completely against the 10 commandments.

    a. It violates the commandment thou shalt not steal. Confiscating the wealth of people who earned it and saved it is stealing.

    b. The people who vote for this kind of crap are violating the commandment thou shalt not covet they neighbor's goods.

    c. Warn herself violates the commandment that says thou shalt not bear false witness against my neighbor. She is lying about the wealth of people who have worked extremely hard and saved their money for the well-being of themselves and their families. She actively hates and demonizes these kinds of people.

    This woman is as far from being Christian as you can get without being murderous or an atheist in my opinion. This is all because Warren feels it's not fair to other people that you gain money on your investments. This is what she will do to your IRA and all other investments as well. This is nothing more than long-term government confiscation of everybody's wealth. It is in this way that she plans to willfully and purposely destroy all your sacrifices and work in order to increase your health and well-being through the money you have saved for decades.

Anybody who is supporting this idea is doing so out of pure jealousy and envy. It is the old story of the have-nots wanting to confiscate the wealth of the haves. If we go down this road, pretty soon the haves will have nothing left to tax and Warren will have achieved her grandiose goal of equality for all. But the equality everybody shares is one of abject poverty and all the health and well-being problems that come with that.

Margaret Thatcher, Prime Minister of the United Kingdom famously said that socialism works for a while until you run out of other people's money that you confiscate from them. Pocahontas Elizabeth Warren will bring horrific lower standards of living in our country. And this is just one of her idiot ideas to **destroy** the United States as we know it.

2. Warren has a proposed policy called the "accountable capitalism act". This is a real bomb that will explode in every citizens face. One of the rules in this false monstrosity is she will force companies to take large sums of their profits and instead of giving it to the owners of the company called shareholders, she will force them to give it to her favorite list of recipients. This completely destroys the mechanism of free market capitalism that is made this country great and has put food in everyone's mouth closed on everyone's back and a roof over everyone's head. And if you are now thinking about the homeless situation and saying no capitalism is failed, you are completely wrong. All the homeless in this country reside in cities that have been governed by Democrats for a long time and are a result, a direct result of their socialist policies. It is the same policies that Warren wants to distribute across the entire country and as a result our entire country will end up looking like the filthy drug infested, poop infested streets of San Francisco that are littered with used needles and tents clogging the cities sidewalks.

If you have any kind of retirement plan, this proposal will destroy any prospect you think you have for retiring and using your money in your IRA. Investment values are built upon the profit they make. If you cut the prophet in half so too will the value of the investment go down by half. This is simple economics that the socialist ideologue Elizabeth Pocahontas Warren wants to force upon the people of our country. The word stupid does not scratch the surface of the depth of the heinous results of doing something so completely disastrous like this.

Socialists like Pocahontas Warren do not only redistribute and confiscate wealth, they completely destroy it. There is only equality in poverty, pain, suffering and death as history shows that happens 100% of the time with socialism.

Bernie Sanders:

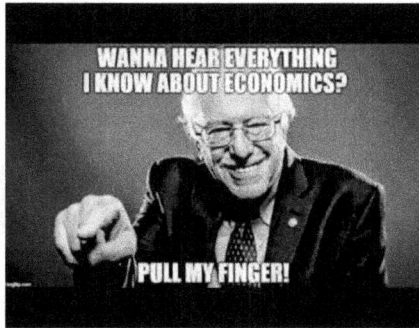

"When you're white, you don't know what it's like to be living in a ghetto. You don't know what it's like to be poor. You don't know what it's like to be hassled when you walk down the street or when you get dragged out of a car." Bernie Sanders Democrat Debate March 2019

Gee I guess there are no white poor or wealthy black people. Racist stereotyping here. Remember, it is not accidental that Bernie's initials are BS.

This idiot has been a socialist monger, a communist radical ever since his early days in this life. So much so that this creature spent his honeymoon in Moscow discussing the finer points of communism with communist government officials. Psychologically, this guy is so far gone he actually believes the BULSHOOT he talks about.

Everything I discussed above regarding Elizabeth Pocahontas Warren applies to this over the hill communist ideologue that has absolutely no concept and no understanding of the way God has created this universe and this earth we live on. This guy is a hostile atheist so what he expect? This creature is nothing more than another of Satan's ignorant minions spreading social and economic disease in our country. It is my belief that this man cannot and does not have the ability to think clearly beyond what is in his canned communist speeches. He talks about fairness and equality yet I read an article with a picture taken by another passenger on an airplane flight where both he and his wife were flying on that aircraft. Bernie was in first class. His wife was in coach. This is Bernie's idea of equality. Get the picture? This human creature is doing his best to spread lies, confusion, and other false talking points in order to gain his lifelong dream of dominion over God's children in the United States. I do not say this in an idle manner just to be nasty. I am committed to the truth of things and this is the truth as best as I can possibly perceive it and discern it through the lens of Judeo-Christian principles and ethics.

Joe Biden:

Hey Baby, I am the vice president you smell really good, hmm hmm good!

Joe Biden has chronic foot in mouth disease. He also cannot keep his hands off of little boys and girls and other people's wives. He is a gaffe machine that just keeps on giving. On this level alone, do we want a president that averages more than one gaffe per day negotiating with hostile foreign powers in order to defuse potential war situations. Comparing Joe with Pres. Trump please remember Trump's first day in office. North Korea was testing nuclear bombs and Intercontinental ballistic missiles. After Pres. Trump implemented his strategy of negotiations have you noticed that there are no more ICBM tests and no more nuclear bomb tests. Additionally, the prospects for peace have increased greatly. Although there is no guarantee on anything the situation today is far much better than it was when Pres. Trump took office. Now, put uncle Joe the gaffe machine in the same situation. Does anyone honestly believe that he would've achieve the same results in avoiding an unconscionable number of deaths due to war where South Korea would probably lose at least 1 million people after North Korea invades.

On another level is becoming increasingly clear that "creepy Joe" may be entering into old age dementia or some other related brain incapacitation. Do we want somebody like that in the Oval Office? Democrats have tried to attach this accusation on to Pres. Trump in their never ending one lie per minute program.

Joe's racism is almost funny were it not hurtful to a lot of people. Here are some examples from his recent public appearances. [32]

---

[32] https://hotair.com/archives/john-s-2/2019/06/14/students-surprised-joe-bidens-awkward-quotes/

"You cannot go into a 7-11 or a Dunkin Donuts unless you have a slight Indian accent. I'm not joking."

"They're going to put y'all back in chains," spoken to a diverse audience including black Americans.

"I mean, you got the first mainstream African-American who is articulate and bright and clean and a nice-looking guy," in reference to Barack Obama.

Can you imagine the disasters this idiot Democrat would make if given the power of the presidency? I have said this before and I will say it again.

Kamala Harris:

Kamala Harris certainly smiles more than the other Democrat candidates for president. However, she is a would be tyrant. It is my opinion that she strongly feels that she knows far better how to run your life than you do. It pretty much boils down to that.

Positions:

Kamala is completely against children of God being able to protect ourselves using guns.

In favor of killing babies right up to being born. Bill De Blasio wants to kill they even after birth. You know, it's a woman's right to kill her baby now isn't it. Too bad her parents disagreed.

Wants increased federal taxes from you so as to pay for far larger social and medicare for illegal aliens. First time I heard a Democrat admit taxpayers will pay the bill for illegal aliens. Normally they just ignore talking about it.

Is against lower business taxes to promote higher economic growth

Totally in favor of the idiotic Green New Deal which will completely destroy our economy and social structures. So ignorant I do not believe she can even spell the word economics. Bet she does not even know the difference between micro and macroeconomics. Sad for all of us.

"Upon being elected, I will give the United States Congress 100 days to get their act together and have the courage to pass reasonable gun safety laws and if they fail to do it, then I will take executive action and specifically what I would do is put in a requirement for anyone who sells more than five guns a year, they are required to do background checks when they sell those guns," she said Monday. "I will require for any gun dealer that breaks the law, the ATF take their license."

Of course, to my knowledge, this is already the law. First, she is flogging the wrong horse. The vast majority of crime is when criminals get illegal guns. Tightening the noose around the necks of already law abiding people does nothing but make her feel good and get headlines.

Wants to confiscate your guns. Period. Don't let her lie and fool you on this.

Wants to put methane collectors on all cows and steers and bulls. Boy, the farm is getting morphed into a circus. Farmers should now sell tickets to see the big collection bags on cows get so full they either explode or the cow floats away.

She hates the southern wall. She truly believes that your stuff is "their stuff". Never mind it is only you that has earned it and is indeed rightfully yours. Charity begins in the home, not monster government programs forced on its Citizens against their will. That is confiscation.

When asked if she is in favor of free health care for people illegally in the United States, Harris said, "I'm opposed to any policy that would deny any human being from access to public safety, public education, or public health. Period." In other words, Kamala Harris sees no difference between a taxpaying US citizen and an illegal alien. It gets worse. Due to our tax policies, illegal aliens stand in line ahead of US taxpayers for their earned income. This is what Kamala Harris thinks of us taxpayer people.

There is an underlying feeling going on here. Cory Booker touched on it. He said that our founding fathers were bigots and racists. That our founding documents were racist in their origin. I ask everyone to read our founding documents to see if you can find and racist terms in them. You cannot. You will find Cory Booker to be a liar. Instead there are expressions of love of people and country. But facts do not deter people like Kamala Harris. Because she thinks we are a racist nation, we must pay the health bills of anyone who is her illegally. Just that simple. Who pays? You do!

It is very possible that Kamala Harris will be the running mate of Creepy Joe Biden in the 2020 Election. Beware and pay attention. Either her or Elizabeth Pocahontas Warren have a great shot at the vice presidential nomination with "Where am I" Biden.

If you vote Democrat in 2020, you will need to go to a proctologist in order to get your head examined.

Part Three

Socialism, System of Suffering, Pain and Death

The great manifestation of socialist Satan in the United States

Democrats and The Sacred Ten Commandments:

A lot of ignorant people think that the 10 Commandments are there only to spoil the party of life. To take away all the fun stuff. For democrats having fun is their only real goal of life, the objective of life is to have as good a time as possible all the time. And these damned 10 Commandments do really get in the way of that. In fact, I bet 10 out of 10 people you meet on the street cannot even list five of the 10 Commandments even after thinking about it and concentrating for a while.

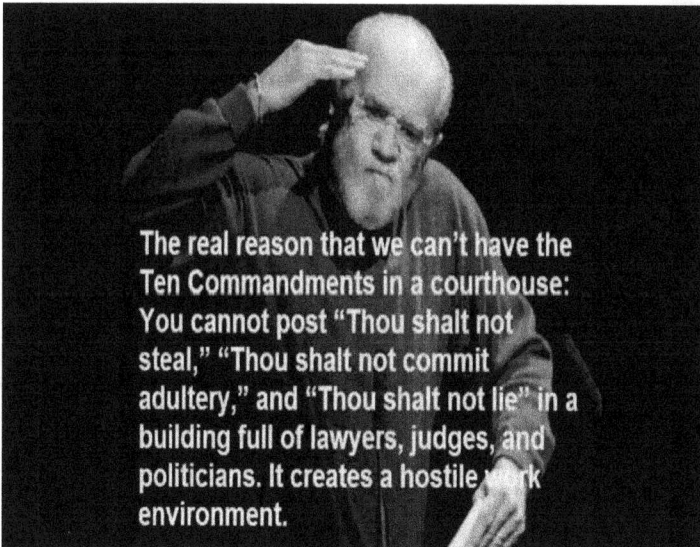

The real reason that we can't have the Ten Commandments in a courthouse: You cannot post "Thou shalt not steal," "Thou shalt not commit adultery," and "Thou shalt not lie" in a building full of lawyers, judges, and politicians. It creates a hostile work environment.

George Carlin Comedian and Poet. One of the Best

The 10 commandments are not a cosmic party pooper. They are not the result of the universe being a big meanie against fun. They are not the Castor oil of life. Once you understand life and universal Christian existential philosophy, you will understand that the 10 Commandments are your keys to the kingdom of eternal joy and happiness with Almighty God. This last sentence could be the most important sentence you have ever read in your entire life. So here it is again.

The 10 Commandments are your keys to the kingdom of eternal joy and happiness with Almighty God. They are also your keys to living a fulfilled joyful life here on earth.

As Christians we always must be diligent to the policies of government and measure the worth of them using Christian foundational principles. We must always remember that for every political issue there are two sides of every coin. Politicians like to only talk about the one side they like ignoring all the rest. For example, opposition to the border wall has another violent and expensive side to it with MS 13 killing more and more American citizens. In light of this government has totally, willfully and purposely failed in its number one duty which is to protect us from harm.

Let's take a look at each commandment and compare that with our satanically driven Democrat party. And as a reminder I am not speaking about every day normal people who vote Democrat because they're too ignorant to know any better. They're not evil, they are just stupidly ignorant and have a disease I call "**constipation of the corpus callosum**". This is a sophisticated medical term that simply means the left half of your brain doesn't know the right half is there and the right half of your brain does not know the left half is there.

Satan and the Democratic Party:

I do not condemn all Democrats. The vast majority of Democrat voters are regular people struggling with everyday life as all of us do. Serious problems arise however when anybody and I do mean anybody does not take the time to understand workings of this world. Then you become ignorant and can be manipulated easily by Democrat lies about everything. Most people do not understand their own psychology and weaknesses that they have as individual people. Most people do not understand the completely vicious nature of national politics in general. Most people are not in tune with the political agendas of the Democrat party. Most people do not have the time to understand the objective truth that it exists within our beloved country. Most people are simply ignorant of the evil agendas that exist within all levels of our government, federal, state and local.

This condition of not understanding and not knowing brings about a fertile playground for Satan and politicians with hidden agendas that in devious ways to undermine the health and well-being of American citizens and the country as a whole. As communist radical Saul Alinsky has said, it is far easier to manipulate people when they don't know what's going. They will fall for the appropriate political manipulation of them to behave and vote in ways he wants them to. This is in his book, "Rules for Radicals". It is an awful book of how to perform manipulation and deception people.

In many different ways Democrat leadership can be very vile creatures posing as compassionate human beings. As an example, all Democrats presidential candidates want to give away free college, free Medicare and a host of other expensive benefits to everybody in the United States. This outrageously includes everybody that is here illegally called illegal aliens. This means theoretically anybody in the world from any country can come here, claim asylum what ever reason and Democrats will give them all the benefits you can imagine for free. This is what's known as the bait. The bait always sounds really good and desirable.

Democrats never tell you who pays free stuff and the economic negative impact will have on American citizens who will indeed pay for this from their own sacred productive lives in the form of taxes that will go ever higher and higher along with a far larger central Government wants to control every aspect of our lives.

I have observed for a very long time now the politics of the United States. My observations started in the 1960s during the Vietnam War. I was an Army ROTC cadet in college. It looked like I was going to end up being a Second Lieutenant in Vietnam. Needless to say, I was very interested in the politics of the times hoping I would not have to go there. As it turns out I didn't. Thank you Lord for that.

One of the things I observed early on was the Democrat party and its connection with the KKK. Democrat Sen. Robert Byrd is a shining example of the tight connections between the Democrat party and its racist anti-black heritage in the history of our country. Early on after the Civil War that freed all slaves in the United States it was the Republican Party, the party of Abraham Lincoln, that the Blacks in our country voted for. It was the Democrats that were the racists and they are the ones that instituted such things as the Jim Crow laws.

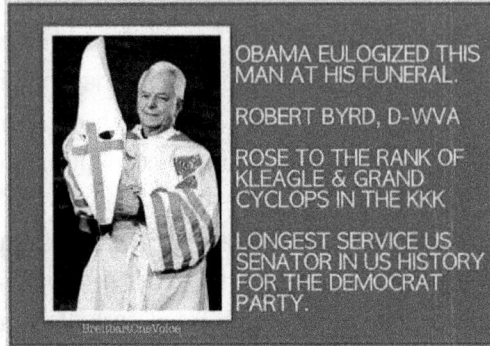

OBABA EULOGIZED THIS MAN AT HIS FUNERAL.

ROBERT BYRD, D-WVA

ROSE TO THE RANK OF KLEAGLE & GRAND CYCLOPS IN THE KKK

LONGEST SERVICE US SENATOR IN US HISTORY FOR THE DEMOCRAT PARTY.

This Satanic Minion is the Real Thing. Hates everybody especially blacks. Obama and Clinton love him though. Did you vote for these three?

These connections between anti-black racism in the Democrat party have extended even into the Obama administration. Obama said glowing congratulatory words about the racist Senator Byrd when he gave the eulogy at Sen. Byrd's funeral. There is even a picture of Hillary Clinton kissing Sen. Byrd with a smile on her face.

Can you really believe that both Barack Obama and Hillary Clinton believe in what they say about racism? Both these two human beings disgust me for all their lies, deceit and crass manipulation of people who ignorantly put their faith into these two Satan's minions.

The Satan Inspired Great Democrat Party Lie About America:

Based on the rhetoric that is constantly used by Democrat politicians it is clear to this writer that the radical liberals in the Democratic Party are using the very same tactic that Satan used to convince Adam and Eve to "eat the apple of the knowledge of good and evil". This was against the rules that God laid down for them. Because of this act of rebellion death now became inevitable for them, their children and all of their descendants in human history.

The garden of Eden was created for humankind. In it was ever so many delicious and healthy sources of food for Adam and Eve. There was only one tree that God expressly forbid them to eat from, the tree of the knowledge of good and evil. For both Adam and Eve knew that if they ate from that tree they would surely die. This is what God expressly told them. This tree was only one tree out of ever so many trees that populated the garden. Everything in the garden was wonderful beyond our contemporary imaginations.

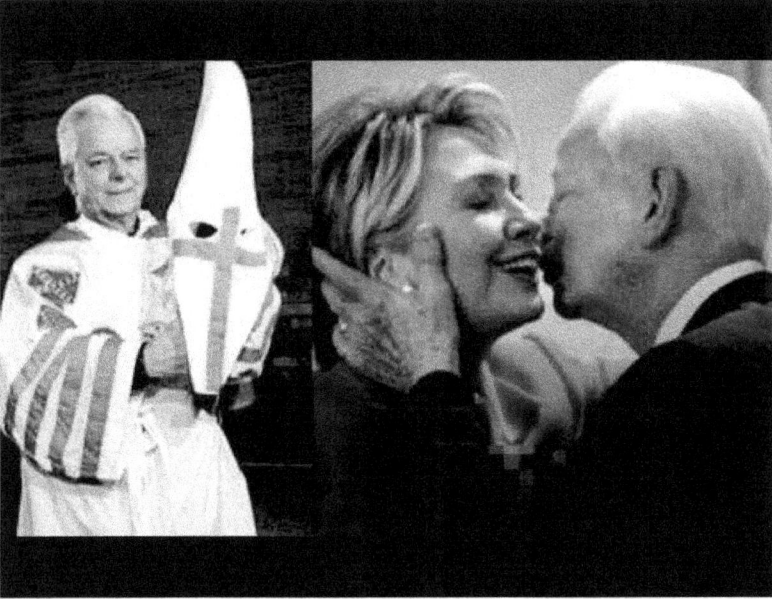

Oh...lovie dovie smoochie smoochie with Robert Byrd

Satan appeared to them as a snake. The snake must have been beautiful for Eve became very curious upon seeing it. Notice that Satan hid his real identity as the author of all lies and death. He disguised himself which in and of itself that action is a lie. Satan then told Eve that eating from the tree of the knowledge of good and evil would make them like God himself. Satan said you will surely not die. These are two of the biggest lies ever spoken in human history for believing these two lies all of human history and God's children has been altered permanently.

Satan took the one and only temptation laid before Adam and Eve and sold the idea to Adam and Eve that God was a liar. Satan said God lied to them when he told them that they would surely die if they ate from that single tree in the garden. He lied that they would become like God. He lied about his own appearance as a snake for surely if Satan appeared to them in his natural state they would never believe a word that he said to them.

Satan had a hidden agenda. Satan lied about who he was. Satan lied about the tree of the knowledge of good and evil. Satan accused Almighty God of being the liar. So, you have the author of all lies, deceit, death and destruction lying about God being a liar. In the history of mankind after Adam and Eve, Satan has become the accuser that works against all of God's children. He accuses each of us of all our sins and argues that we should never be allowed into the kingdom of God, what we call heaven.

The Great Democrat Lie:

I have observed that the Democrat leadership, Democrats in general, the radical leftist Democrats and the Democratic National Committee have all adopted the very same tactics that Satan used on Adam and Eve. If we as a country believe these liars and Masters of deceit, our country as we know it will surely die. There will be far more pain, suffering and death within our great country if we believe the lies and deceit that the Democrat party constantly propagandize is about.

Just like Satan, the Democrat party poses as a force for good and is "fighting the evil of democracy, the evil white racists and supremacists and the United states of America as a whole".

There are a number of lies we are constantly told by the Democrat party.

The Satan Inspired Great Democrat Party Lies

1. The United States is a racist nation
2. The Democrat Party has all the answers
3. The United States is an illegitimate country because we were founded on the backs of slaves and genocide.
4. Our country is controlled by white supremacists, greedy, rich people, corporations and racists
5. Our country and our economy discriminate against people of color on a systemic and widespread basis
6. If you are a white person, you are automatically a racist.
7. If you are a white male, then you automatically are a white supremacist.
8. Barack Obama said we are no longer a Christian nation. Remember Obama is a Muslim.
9. Democracy does not work for everybody, only the rich.
10. Our economy is designed only for the benefit of rich people and by definition rich people can always be counted as evil.
11. National borders to control who is in our country is in and of itself a terrible evil.
12. Wealthy people do not pay their fair share in taxes, actually they pay more
13. Donald Trump is an illegal president

14. People of foreign origin residing here illegally are not illegal at all, rather they are only undocumented. America is cruel to enforce our immigration policies.

15. Anybody who manages to slip across our border is automatically guaranteed the rights of a citizen even though they are completely illegal being here. These illegal aliens have a superior right to the productive lives of American citizens in the form of free healthcare, free food and free shelter paid for by the American taxpayer. In this way they are superior in the eyes of radical Democrats to normal American citizens. We are terrible people if we question this.

16. Special Democrat lie to black citizens: Only us Democrats care about your awful plight in this world. You need us to fight for your rights and compensate you for all the evil the white man has done to you. Never mind that we started the KKK, never mind we wrote the Jim Crow laws, never mind that since the 1960's Civil Rights bill and the uncountable billions spent on "disadvantaged" areas, you still are not one whit better off because of things like we oppose school vouchers etc. See, we plan to keep you right where you are.

17. Christians are unfit for high political office like in the court system. Because of separation of church and state we must separate Christians from holding political offices

18. Global warming is the #1 priority for government. We will all die unless Democrats win in 2020 and are given the political power to completely destroy our current economic structures, current social order and current policies in favor of a hyper monster sized government to fund a completely New Society based on socialism

19. We must get rid of combustion engines, eliminate airplanes, eliminate most all vehicles, eliminate ships, rebuild ALL existing buildings to new harsh regulations,

20. We must eliminate the difference between the status of "American citizen" and "illegal alien". Everyone everywhere has US constitutional rights including the right to vote in all our elections.

21. We must accept Islam as it is a religion of peace. Christianity must be dealt with and reduced.

22. We must raise taxes

23. We must impeach President Donald Trump

24. The United States was NEVER all that great.

25. We must get rid of both the first and second amendments in the Bill of Rights, the right to free speech and the right to bear arms. Free speech hurts people's feelings, guns kill thousands every year. We need to stop "gun violence".
26. We Democrats are the party of equality of result.

Source: The American Thinker [33]

Additionally, over the past 90 years virtually all potential oligarchs or tyrants have utilized the following six political stratagems, that do not require armed conflict, in order to permanently obliterate any opposition. They were first employed by Adolf Hitler and documented by renowned American Psychoanalyst, Dr. Walter C Langer:

Keep the public in a state of constant turmoil. Pre-identify favored groups by race, economic status, ideology or religion and through constant repetition by allies in the media and entertainment cabal, establish that any perceived disadvantage within those assemblages is solely the fault of another pre-identified and isolated group, particularly Jews, traditional Christians and the capitalists.

Never concede that there may be some good in your political enemy. State loudly and often that they are a permanent adversary because they are determined to oppress the favored groups identified in 1) above as well as being racist, avaricious, treasonous etc. (i.e. the worst people on earth). Thus, abrogation of their free speech privileges, their right to own firearms and to freely assemble is not only acceptable but a necessity.

Never miss an opportunity to repeatedly and loudly blame one's political enemy for anything that goes wrong regardless of how inane or unreasonable. Thus, faux crises must be orchestrated as often as possible in order to blame the other side. Further, any natural disaster or any aggressive action by a foreign adversary must also be attributed to one's political adversary.

Never acknowledge or divulge that your side is at fault or wrong regardless of the situation or issue.

Never, under any circumstances, leave room for civil discourse regarding alternative societal or governmental policies by proclaiming that those promoting any alternative have a hidden treasonous agenda. Continually maintain the assertion as being irrefutable

---

33
https://www.americanthinker.com/articles/2019/06/where_the_democrats_are_trying_to_take_us.html#ixzz5tE9qegjt

that a central government, in the hands of the enlightened, can resolve any issue and make life better.

Finally, always utilize the ultimate tactic in promoting dogma or denigrating one's opponent: The Big Lie. People will believe a big lie sooner than a little one; and if it is repeated frequently enough, people will sooner or later accept it as the truth. The fabricated dire consequences of so-called climate change; the contrived narrative of Donald Trump colluding with Russia; the myth of rampant white nationalism and the illusion that this is a virulently racist nation are recent examples of this stratagem.

Comparing the 10 Commandments with the Democrat party:

1. "I am the Lord thy God, thou shalt not have any strange gods before Me." Simply put this forbids idolatry of any kind. When it comes to strange gods this means far more than just golden cabs as in the Old Testament with Moses or other man-made clay idols. The general meaning is that a pagan God for example can be anything that you worship as your God. This could be another person, it could be a lifestyle that is detrimental to your health and well-being, or it could be any number of things like what the Democrats worship. For many people it is money. Money is a great magnet of sin when it comes to idolatry. Money is a powerful tool to be used wisely and for the good as defined by Almighty God. Democrats worship other people's money. They promise a lot of free stuff which requires much more money to flow into the coffers of the government so they can spend it any way they choose including giving away so-called" free stuff", which anybody with more than two brain cells rubbing together realizes it's as a complete lie.

   Bernie Sanders goes into a bar and yells, "free drinks for everybody!"
   After many drinks are served Bernie then asks, "so who's going to pay?"

   Because of Democrats obsession with climate it is reasonable to say that one of their gods is the earth and climate. In very ancient times when mankind did not understand that all of his environment, he did worship the sun, the earth, the air, and fire. There is no excuse for acting like this is true today. The crime of this is that they put their perverted needs of their god Gaia above the real needs of the sacred children of Almighty God.

   Democrats worship a monster sized government. They view the government as taking care of all the needs of the people and structure the society in such a way that everybody shares equally in the poverty that exists 100% of the time in socialist countries. Hundreds of millions of people have endured pain, suffering and have because of socialism. Socialist government is for certain the pagan God they put above our Judeo-Christian Almighty God Creator of heaven and earth and of all that is seen and unseen. These people are just plain nuts. These Democrat leaders who promote socialism have absolutely no concept of where they are in the universe. They have no concept that the spirit realm is far more powerful than the physical. They ignorantly fall into Satan's trap of hubris where they think each of them are many gods that just have to say the right things and promise enough free stuff to gain power and dominion over the rest of God's children.

Democrats worship Socialism and the Democrat party says there is no Almighty God at all. In their satanic minds, they think a huge central government is God. Said differently they think they are God because they seek dominion and control over God's real children and will command every aspect of human life. This is precisely what Satan lusted after before he was thrown out of the kingdom of God.

If they want things like Satan, if they do things like Satan, if they lust for things like Satan, chances are excellent they are Satan's minions. Following orders from Satan through their misguided feelings with no brain insight.

Also remember this:

In effect their worship of monster government is in actuality worshiping themselves. For it is they worship government and want to be the monster government. This is idolatry pure and simple in its most heinous and vile form. This is precisely what Satan wanted which is to worship himself.
Not only is this a heinous sin of self worship with Socialism against God but it has failed miserably 100% of the time in human history. Why?
The farther you move away from God's love and commandments the more pain, suffering and death come to those who do this. Socialism/Communism are prime examples.

Many tens of millions of innocent people have died under the yoke of communism and socialism and the laws are Democrat party wants to implement to control us. God has given us freedom as individuals, but Democrats view us only as a cog in a big wheel with no freedom except that which is granted by the monster government, they think is God which is really themselves have total power over the people. Just like the lusts Satan has. Socialism and the Democrat party are working hard to accomplish the very thing that Satan failed to do in the heavenly realm by gaining dominion over all creation. Guess who is going to hell these days. Pray for these idiots. They really need it badly.

2.   "Thou shalt not take the name of the Lord thy God in vain."

One of the most shocking and disgusting displays of atheism occurred when Democrats booed Almighty God at their national convention in 2012. I was watching TV when this happened. I remember it well. I wanted to puke on my TV. Confession time, I flipped off my TV screen in a fit of anger against these future residents of hell. [34] According to pew research, approximately 70% of the atheists in the United States are Democrats. What does this tell you about their moral values and their complete absence of Judeo-Christian principles?

"Democrats need to remember that God's last name is not dammit."

And it is these people that want to run our country. I think the word is more like ruin instead of run. These people are useful idiots as Karl Marx would say. As a pastoral minister I would say that Satan is firmly entrenched in their minds and their heart and he controls what they say and do while allowing them to think they have freedom. They already have 1 foot in hell as it is.

3.   "Remember to keep holy the Sabbath day."

We know that Democrats do not keep the Sabbath holy. Since they do not recognize Almighty God, they will certainly not keep the Sabbath day holy for they themselves are not holy. What a tragedy. Bet they cannot even spell Sabbath.

4.   "Honor thy father and mother."

This is something that cannot be commented on for it is highly personal and depends on individual family circumstances. However, I can make only one comment from a lifetime of observations of people in the political realm. Politicians cannot be trusted no matter which party they are affiliated with. The headlines in our news media continue to be full of dishonesty in marital affairs and other family issues. I am hoping that I am completely wrong but it appears

---

[34]   https://www.dailywire.com/news/31913/democrats-boo-god-then-they-quote-bible-attack-michael-j-knowles

to me that honoring mothers and fathers is not high on the priority list of people in the Democrat party leadership.

I include in this commandment to honor your wife. Marriage means to becoming one and of course many other things. It is the measure of a person how they treat their parents and their spouse.

A terrible example is Bernie Sanders. Elsewhere in this book I mentioned how he treated his wife on a commercial flight. There are pictures of him in first class taken by another passenger and put on the Internet. Guess where Bernie's wife was. She was somewhere way back in coach while Bernie sipped wine with the white tablecloth and other goodies she had her choice of coffee tear milk and maybe a Coke and water. I do not believe anybody wants to be Bernie Sanders wife. He never smiles either when he gives speeches. He like many other Democrats do not know how to smile. Do you want to know why? It is because Satan really never smiles either. He certainly has nothing to smile about.

5. "Thou shalt not kill."

Democrats love to use this commandment when they are pontificating about wanting to confiscate all our guns. They have taken a particular hate toward a medium powered rifle called an AR-15. NO, "AR" does NOT stand for "assault rifle" like ignorant Democrats want you to believe. It stands for "Armalite" the manufacture of the first in the series of Armalite rifles.

FACT: STATISTICALLY YOU ARE MORE LIKELY TO BE KILLED BY HILLARY CLINTON THAN BY AN AR 15 [35]

This is an absolutely huge and important commandment. A better translation of this fifth commandment should be "thou shalt not murder" as in what Cain did to Able. There is something that needs to be understood regarding this commandment as it applies to politics. It is my belief and perception that this commandment also applies to willful and purposeful policies put into law by people in government. For example:

a. Our federal government has ignored the awful situation at our border with Mexico. Multiple presidents ignored the monster inflows of dangerous drugs into our country that we all know have killed many hundreds of thousands of people over the years. This is a well-known

[35] https://www.freedomwatchusa.org/statistically-you-are-more-likely-to-be-killed-by-hillary-cl

fact and yet the Bush administration, the Clinton administration and the Obama administration looked the other way did nothing.

This is tantamount of saying they watched people being killed and did nothing about it. This is complicity to murder.

It is only Pres. Trump that has done his level best to fix this murderous situation.

But, the entire Democratic Party has done everything possible to prevent him from fixing the murderers that are going on through drugs, through human trafficking and wars between drug cartels.

Democrats actually hate President Trump for attempting to heal our southern border and protect American Citizens.

Democrats have turned their backs on protecting American citizens from murder and other crimes.

b.   The better translation from the Hebrew would be "Thou shalt not murder" — a subtle distinction but an important one to the Church. Killing an innocent person is considered murder. Killing an unjust aggressor to preserve your own life is still killing, but it isn't considered murder or immoral. Now what about abortion?

Abortion is murder. That deserves to be repeated. Abortion is murder. It can be nothing else but murder. It involves a willful and purposeful killing of an innocent developing fetal human being in a sacred place called a mother's womb. Scientifically speaking and morally speaking life begins at conception, there is no other truth than this. A fertilized human egg meets all the scientific criteria of being alive and being human. Not believing this sacred truth and violating this commandment leads to stories like the following one.

More Than 2,200 Preserved Fetuses Found at Property of Dead Doctor, Officials Say: [36]

The family of a doctor in Illinois discovered more than 2,200 medically preserved fetuses at his property a little over a week after his death, the authorities said.

Source: The New York Times Sept 14, 2019

How any more heinous can you get? This story makes me sick to my stomach but here it is. What is even more sickening is that this story is completely consistent with the Democrat Party Platform.

EVERY DEMOCRAT PRESIDENTIAL CANDIDIATE SUPPORTS WHAT IT TOOK TO GATHER 2,200 DEAD BABIES AT THAT MONSTER DOCTOR'S HOME.

So, does anyone still want to vote Democrat now?

If anybody tells you different, they are either completely ignorant, or they are lying about it and are part of Satan's Democrat squadron of minions trying to miss name things in order to promote heinous crime against God's children and Almighty God himself. It is my opinion that anybody that purposely and willfully distorts this truth is a future resident of hell. Does anybody want to bet me where Margaret's anger is? I will bet anybody $10,000 no make that $1 million if they can prove that Margaret's Sanger is not in hell right now. If you are unwilling to take this bet, then that tells me there is some amount of truth rattling around inside your brain and your heart. This is a good thing for it shows there is hope for you from a Judeo-Christian spiritual perspective.

c. Murder also includes not only physical murder and ending a person's physical life but it also includes killing a person's future, killing their God given inner gifts such as intellectual abilities, social abilities and psychological assets that can enhance not only their lives but also the

---

[36] https://www.nytimes.com/2019/09/14/us/dr-ulrich-klopfer-fetal-remains.html

lives of those who come into contact with the person if the murder of their inner well being never took place.

In our society today we call it by such terms as child abuse, sexual abuse, child pornography, child trafficking for sex, enslavement and the list goes on. All these acts murder the inner person and kill their life's potential as was ordained by Almighty God.

On glaring example has been recently exposed with Jeffery Epstein who was supposedly committed suicide inside the highest security prison in our country. Did he kill himself? BULLSHOOTY!!! This creep ran a child prostitution ring which involved transporting high level politicians and business people on his private jet called the "Lolita Express" to his private island called "Pedophile Island" in the Bahamas.

Guess who was one of Epstein's biggest customers, Bill Clinton.

The Washington Times [37]

Bill Clinton ditched Secret Service on multiple 'Lolita Express' flights: Report September 20, 2019

"Flight logs obtained by Gawker in January 2015 put Mr. Clinton on the billionaire's infamous jet more than a dozen times — sometimes with a woman whom federal prosecutors suspect of
procuring underage sex victims for Mr. Epstein. Fox News reported Friday that records show Mr. Clinton declined Secret Service protection on at least five flights.

The network's investigation reveals Mr. Clinton flew on the Boeing 727 "Lolita Express" 26 times, more than doubling the previously reported 11 trips."

---

[37]   https://www.washingtontimes.com/news/2016/may/14/bill-clinton-ditched-secret-service-on-multiple-lo/

This is just one example of Democrats and their sexual perversions that are finally coming to light. Expect more filth to hit the news over the next year or so. These sexual escapades with very young vulnerable underage girls KILL their mental health and well being to the point that they may never recover from the atrocities committed against them. They are sentenced to a living hell just so wretched people like Bill Clinton can have a sexual thrill for a few hours. There is a special place in hell for Bill and Hillary Clinton.

d. Other pedophile crimes include: [38] (I do not know of any Republicans that are associated with pedophilia. There is something systemic with the mindset of Democrats and a blizzard of sex crimes especially killing the inner being of children. To me this is definitely the work of Satan.)

1. Democratic Seattle Mayor Ed Murray resigned Tuesday after more allegations of child sexual abuse surfaced in what is becoming a disturbing pattern of Democratic politicians involved in crimes and allegations of child sexual abuse — scandals largely ignored by the media.

2. Anthony Weiner: What an appropriate name. "*The disgraced Democratic politician has a long history of sexual misconduct which most recently landed him in legal trouble when he became involved in an online sexual relationship with a 15-year-old girl. Weiner pleaded guilty to transferring obscene material to a minor and faces up to ten years in prison — he also must now register as a sex offender.*" [39]

3. Sen. Robert Menendez (D-NJ): *He is currently on trial facing federal corruption charges, which started in 2012 over allegations that he and another man were having sex with underage prostitutes.*

---

[38] https://www.dailywire.com/news/20982/multiple-democrats-currently-involved-child-sex-ryan-saavedra

[39] https://www.dailywire.com/news/20982/multiple-democrats-currently-involved-child-sex-ryan-saavedra

There are many more Democrats involved with sex crimes both in congress and in support roles such as members of the DNC. Space does not permit more tawdry investigation of these wretched people.

Another form of murder against the inner sacred spirit of children is out right child abuse. Sex is only one form of abuse against children. I have experienced violent abuse against me growing up. Many other children are like me and have to live with PTSD, depression, anhedonia and other very painful emotional damage perpetrated on them when they were a young and their brains for developing. This kind of general abuse is also a form of murder of the inner spirit of God's most innocent, which is the children.

Satan kills the God gifted inner spirit of children through the crimes many Democrat leaders commit against innocent children. This is for sure murder. In the New Testament, Jesus Christ referred to even killing the reputation of someone in the community as murder. There are many more ways to be guilty of murder then killing the physical body.

4. Headline Report: [40] *Ilhan Omar Cheats on Husband, Leaves Him for Political Consultant, Then HAD HIM FIRED from Job Back in Minnesota*

> *New evidence has emerged earlier this week that Rep. Ilhan Omar did indeed marry her brother, and that her real name may actually be Ilhan Nur Said.*

Boy what a nice woman huh. She marries her brother so she can get a green card in the United States. Then she leaves him for some other Democrat wacko. Then she has the Democrat wacko fired from his job in the Democrat party. This woman certainly nuzzles up closely with Satan and her

---

[40]   https://www.blabber.buzz/conservative-news/661374-report-ilhan-omar-cheats-on-husband-leaves-him-for-political-consultant-then-had-him-fired-from-job-back-in-minnesota-special?utm_source=c-mid&utm_medium=c-mid-email&utm_term=c-mid-GI

actions speak louder than words. This is a disgusting human being doing the work of Satan in the Democrat party.

Having your lover fired from his job in the Somalia district of Minnesota is a form of character assassination. As said above Jesus Christ considers this a form of murder.

6. "Thou shalt not commit adultery."

The sixth and ninth commandments honor human sexuality. This commandment forbids the actual, physical act of having immoral sexual activity, specifically adultery, which is sex with someone else's I spouse or a spouse cheating on their partner. This commandment also includes *fornication,* which is sex between unmarried people, prostitution, pornography, homosexual activity, masturbation, group sex, rape, incest, pedophilia, bestiality, and necrophilia.

If there is one thing besides lying, treachery, dishonesty and other awful things, politicians are all famous for committing adultery. All we have to think of is Bill Clinton. Did you know that wild Bill Hick-Cock was on Lolita express to pedophilia Island owned by his long-term friend and good buddy Jeffrey Epstein? They certainly weren't going they are to meditate and have discussions on biblical literature. Hillary Clinton is just as guilty with her more strategically hidden boyfriends. These two occupied the fast lane on the highway to hell. Rightly so.

Now here is a popular sin. Our entertainment industry seems to be based on violence and adultery. Gee, what would our movies be like if there was no killing and then hopping in the sack with a beautiful woman to celebrate. Okay, please understand I am a very well-seasoned citizen that has observed the degradation of the moral standards that you still exist in this country. You have my permission to call me an old fart. However, I have made use of this time on earth to learn as much as I can about very many things. This certainly qualifies to be as an objective opinion source on quite a number of topics, sex included. In the last 50 years the moral standards of the United States have disintegrated to the lowest level I can imagine. Well, it's not imagination it's more of a nightmare.

It used to be when people got shot on TV or in the movies you never saw blood. That was understood. Now the bloodier, the more gore the more body parts flying through the air the more decapitations in the more let's say creative ways of killing people have been illuminating our movie screens. To a lesser extent TV. But the basic plot lines are the same. It can be summarized by saying "FU!" This covers the landscape of FU I will kill you or FU in a more literal sense with love to be found nowhere in sight.

Hollywood promotes this garbage every minute of every day in every week of every year. They will tell us that they are only providing what we want. Well...BULLSHOOTY!!! Hollywood has no morals and that is now reflected in recent years by their complete antagonism toward Christianity, toward moral values and anything that gives real meaning to life in a gentle and loving way. This is the easy way out for Hollywood because it does not take any morality or imagination to stage an explosion that blows up a bunch of people and then call it entertainment.

My new name for Hollywood is now willfully and purposely changed to "HELLYWOOD". In my opinion all the actors and actresses that people fawn over already have 10 toes in hell. In fact that would be a good movie title for a movie about people who do go to hell. Hollywood is well on the way and has already paved the highway for themselves and everyone else.

The really morbid sin from Hollywood is that they make violence, they make hatred and other Satanic ideals look like they're really fun and exciting. This is a direct action against the young people in our society who are looking for moral guidance. They go to the movies a lot and what do they see, bang bang boom boom screw you too. And that is their entertainment. Anybody look at a pinball machine lately? Do that sometime and look at the themes. I would like to take their paddle Wacker and smash a few of them. But since I'm a Christian I'll do that gently.

Okay, you have the picture now. Bottom line is this. Flirting is fine. F*cking is not. Unless it is with your wife. This is all very simple. Remember that. Yes, there are gray areas in this topic as well. If a 13 or 14-year-old testosterone filled boy named Richard wants to play with his nickname in the privacy of his bedroom, I do not believe he's going to hell for that.

Notice how neatly I have avoided all the sexual perversions promoted by the Democrat party. They are like an ice cream shop called 31 flavors. So much kinky and weird to choose from. I would have to write an encyclopedia of sex to cover it all. So, to end this horny topic all I can think of is a city in Thailand and say **"Phuquet"**. Whew! Wasn't that fun.

7. "Thou shalt not steal."

The seventh and tenth commandments focus on respecting and honoring the possessions of others. This commandment forbids the act of taking someone else's property. But this commandment includes more than just stealing other people's physical property. It also includes stealing their God given right of peace of mind, of physical safety, of a reasonable future built on their own hard work, their freedom to believe in the religion that produces the most health and well-being for not only themselves but all those people around them. If a government denies its citizens any of the above rights and more, that amounts to a grotesque theft of the gifts given to all of God's children. There is one terrible and awful example of this which is the presidency of Barry Soweto, popularly known as Barack Obama. Our first and hopefully only Muslim president.

Stealing US citizens safety and peace of mind by Barack Obama:

Over the last year or two there has been significant increases in crimes of all different kinds and levels. With the economy doing so well how can this be? Normally crime goes up when people get desperate and steal money and commit other crimes. Now we have the lowest unemployment level in over 50 years, we have the highest level of employment in our nation's history. Blacks and Hispanics have the lowest level of unemployment in our nation's history as well. Given these facts how is it crime of all kinds is increasing significantly?

The answer is Barack Hussein Obama. Surprised? I understand why you would be. It is because our mainstream media refuses to report this ugly story and the facts around it. If they did report it would look bad for Democrat party policies and specifically Barack Obama and what he did during his presidency. So what did Barack do and why?

Barry a.k.a. Barack reduced the population of our prisons state local and federal by 310,000 felons during his time as president. He simply opened the door and let them out. That is a 15% drop in prison inmates. Now, one plus one equals two. It doesn't take Einstein or Stephen Hawking to figure out that when you let a whole bunch of criminals out loose on the streets you will get an increase in crime of all kinds. That is precisely what has happened. Thank you Barack Obama. As one example, sexual molestation, attack and rape have doubled since Barack Obama became president.

This is the identical thing happening was sanctuary cities. I never thought that our government would actively and fully protect felons from our justice system only because they are illegal aliens. Our country is increasingly flooded with illegal drugs, MS 13 gang members whose motto is "rape, kill and control", and other felons who have been deported but are let back into the country to continue killing and raping innocent American citizens.

This is 100% the fault of the Democrat party whose ideology is socialism. This action also shows and demonstrates completely the Democrat party's hatred of the United States and its Judeo-Christian citizens. This is like waving Satan's flag in

front of everybody. Completely disgusting and if anybody votes Democrat in 2020 they need their head examined.

Now we hear Democrat presidential idiot candidates complaining vociferously about "all the mass incarcerations that must be racially motivated". These morons actually believe that people are in jail due to the color of their skin and not because of committing felonies against others of God's children. This is complete adolescent insanity. Remember in my previous book "Christians alert!" I went into detail about the psychological shortfalls of the Democrat party and Democrat radical leftists in general and how they are psychologically developed only to the level of adolescence. They have not achieved the level of adulthood. Therefore even stupid reasons seem right to them.

So please remember this commandment again stealing also applies to stealing anything that has been given to God's children by Almighty God such as peace of mind and their right for freedom of movement and many other rights of his children.

The Catholic Church believes that this commandment also denounces cheating people of their money or property, depriving workers of their just wage, or not giving employers a full day's work for a full day's pay. Embezzlement, fraud, tax evasion, and vandalism are all considered extensions of violations of the Seventh Commandment.

There is a collision that goes on between this commandment and a Catholic Social doctrine which says that you should obey your government. In case you are worried, the Bible does NOT say that you must obey your government. People get all confused with this. For example, the Bible does not say you must pay your taxes. Jesus did say give unto Caesar that which is Caesar's. Caesar's face was on the coin and the point Jesus was making is that his kingdom has nothing to do with the kingdom of Rome. Thank God for that.

"Unjust laws pose dramatic problems of conscience for morally upright people: when they are called to cooperate in morally evil acts they must refuse. Besides being a moral duty, such a refusal is also a basic human right which, precisely as such, civil law itself is obliged to recognize and protect." [41]

One thing I know for certain. God will not punish us for doing things that are against our free will because we are forced to at the end of the barrel of a gun. This means a whole host of things. When you pay your taxes, the government spends it anyway they want. A significant amount of the time they pay for things that Christians consider immoral and against the 10 commandments. And, Christians are 100% correct.

---

[41] https://www.catholic.org/news/hf/faith/story.php?id=45255

This is an interesting topic because there is no commandment that says you must pay your taxes but if you don't you wind up in jail at the end of the barrel of a gun. That is man-made law not divine law. Our founding fathers actually hated the idea government and classified it as "a necessary evil".

Natural Law:

However, there is also something called natural law. This is very much like the 10 Commandments. But it is expanded to encompass physical reality. According to Wikipedia, natural law asserts that certain rights are inherent by virtue of human nature that is endowed by nature itself which traditionally is Almighty God. We have a human right, a basic inalienable human right to not be forced to break the 10 Commandments. This extends into the right of not having to pay other people to break the 10 Commandments for us, a.k.a. the federal government and state governments of our country.

50 years ago, this was not much of a problem. However, today our government has mutated itself into a monster that does whatever it pleases to enhance its own power over We the People. Because of the IRS we are forced to pay for horrific activities conducted by our government. I will not make a list here because it would be too long and each of us has our own list as well.

For any of you that feel that you are committing sin by paying your taxes knowing a certain amount goes to anti-Christian activities, God does not hold your responsible for that when it goes against your free will. You do not have a free will regarding our government no matter how much they want to trumpet how free we are. So, ugly as it is, give Caesar what Caesar wants and conduct your private lives as stellar, beautiful and exceptional examples of a good clean Christian life. Also, fight against the ever increasing monster government we currently have that is getting only worse and more craven in its Satanic character that spreads across our land.

The bottom line is simply this: taxation is confiscation which equals theft. Governments that use stolen money from its citizens are the ones responsible for what they do. It is not the citizens. God will judge for sure those people in our government that have discretionary power over the money they confiscate from Christians and other God loving people. It is quite possible in my mind that these people I speak of also, like Hollywood, have all 10 toes already in hell.

Lastly remember this. If your toes are in hell, what does that say about the direction you're headed? If you are a Christian, you know the answer. If you are a Democrat, you are scratching your head right now. Enough said.

8. "Thou shalt not bear false witness against thy neighbor."

The Eighth Commandment condemns lying. Because God is regarded as the author of all truth, the Church believes that humans are obligated to honor the truth. The most obvious way to fulfill this commandment is not to *lie* — intentionally deceive another by speaking a falsehood. So, a good Catholic is who you want to buy a used car from.

The one example I will use is the horrific and monstrous amount of lies that I saw on TV during the Russian collusion investigation by William Mueller. It was a 10 ring circus of lies, lies and more lies. There were lies of commission where falsehoods were spoken and there were lies of omission where the truth was just not said. The motivation for all of this was political gain. Said differently it's an attempt to gain dominion over God's children. This is the same damned thing that Satan tried many eons ago and was thrown out of the heavenly realm as a result. Unfortunately, he has been allowed to remain prints of this earth for a limited time which is thankfully coming to an end shortly.

9. "Thou shalt not covet thy neighbor's wife."

The Ninth Commandment forbids the intentional desire and longing for immoral sexuality. To sin in the heart, Jesus says, is to lust after a woman or a man in your heart with the desire and will to have immoral sex with them. Just as human life is a gift from God and needs to be respected, defended, and protected, so, too, is human sexuality. Catholicism regards human sexuality as a divine gift, so it's considered sacred in the proper context — marriage.

As stated before, Democrats have a real problem with all sorts of sex perversions. This includes ignoring the importance of holy matrimony within the sight of Almighty God. Just look at what Ilhan Omar, (real name?) Did regarding marrying her brother to become a US citizen and then leaving him for another Democrat operative. This is one disgusting woman.

I do hate to say this but the Democrats are psychologically adolescent in their nature and if we understand this it is easier for us to see the source of their sexual escapades as motivated by satanic forces that reside inside their heads.

10. "Thou shalt not covet thy neighbor's goods."

The Tenth Commandment forbids the wanting to or taking someone else's property. Along with the Seventh Commandment, this commandment condemns theft and the feelings of envy, greed, and jealousy in reaction to what other people have.

This also applies to freedom. Freedom is indeed a sacred possession that is gifted to all of God's children from the Almighty God Himself. Anyone who unjustly takes away a person's freedom through force is committing a crime against that child of God AND God Himself. Just recently wacko Bill De Blasio just released a law that threatens people that use the term "illegal alien" with a $250,000 fine and perhaps jail too. This goes completely against our Judeo-Christian morality and is yet another example of Satanic dominion lusted after by the likes of liberal Democrat De Blasio.

NYC threatens up to $250G in fines for using terms like 'illegal alien,' threatening to call ICE

So, threatening to call the police is a crime in New York now. Thanks future resident of hell Bill De Blasio!

This is a big one. Our government covets absolutely everything that is owned by God's children, our citizens. When you hear Democrat politicians speak, it is as if they have complete right over deciding how much of your productive life and wealth you have created you get to keep. The government has put themselves first in line for the wealth that you generate by trading part of your sacred life to earn money to provide for yourself, your family and other necessities including charities you decide to support.

The government feels that they are first in line and have made laws to this very same effect. The government spends your money anyway they deem necessary and to hell with you who earned it to begin with. Yes a certain amount of taxes are necessary to fund a vibrant society. In Catholic Christian tradition a 10% tithe is considered sufficient to fund the necessary expenses of keeping a society glued together and functioning properly.

However, the average person who has achieved a high level of earnings through hard work pays approximately 40% or more of their productive life to the government. Simply put this means that:

The government confiscates 40% or more of your sacred productive life that you trade through your work and efforts for money to provide for your family. This confiscation is done with the understanding that government guns back this up against you.

Simply put, the government violates the 10th Commandment in grievous ways every day of every year of your life.

Federal Spending by Welfare Program for Fiscal Years
2018 and 2017 In Billions

Notice the new and very large spending number at the bottom of this page. $375B and $400B in the last two years for "low income individuals and families". This is probably where they hide the spending for the illegal aliens as they are currently flooding our southern border.

One more thing to consider, the numbers you see here are what governments costs to administer these benefits to people. It is NOT the money people actually get. No, remember that there are huge handling costs that occur to confiscate one person's money, administer a mountain of rules and regulations and give your money to someone else. Instinct tells me this government charge is most likely in the 35% to 40% range.

There must be a more efficient way to do this.

Program	Description	FY 2017	FY 2018
Negative Income Tax	EITC and child credit pays cash to families who pay no income tax	79	76
SNAP	Debit cards are distributed to the poor to buy food	70	73
Housing Assistance	Various programs to support low-income housing and development	50	49
SSI	Cash is paid to low-income disabled, blind or senior citizens	56	53
Pell Grants	Financial aid for college tuition, room and board	28	28
TANF	Cash is paid to families as a transition from welfare to work	16	16
Child Nutrition	School lunch, breakfast and after school snacks for school children	22	24
Head Start	Preschool program	10	12
Job Training	Employment services and job training for adults, youth and seniors	6	6
WIC	High protein food for pregnant women and young children	6	6
Child Care	Child care and after school programs	6	6
LIHEAP	Support for utility payments - heating and cooling	2	2
Lifeline	Phone subsidy per household	3	3
	Total of the 13 programs	354	354
Medicaid	Health care for low-income individuals and families	375	400
	Total welfare costs	729	754

One huge argument we must consider. With Bernie Sanders and all the new radical shiny lips liberal Democrat women running around promising free this and free that. Remember two things:

1. Nothing is free. What the government hands out, they have already taken from YOU!
2. Look at that $754 Billion dollar number above. That is what you paid for but NOT what the recipients got. Also remember that the States kick in about $260 billion per year. Therefore, the total spending on welfare programs in the US is about $1 Trillion / year.

In 1959, a mere 60 years ago, the US population was 183 million people. The Federal government total budget back then was a whopping $71 Billion for the whole year. That amounts to $398 of Federal government expense each person on average had to pay for.

Today, in 2019, the US population is 331 million people. The Federal government total budget for this year is $1,101 for each person on average to pay for. This is almost three times the government we had in the 1960's. If you ever wonder why things are so tight in your budget, now you know why. Our government tripled in size and you are paying for all of it. The way things are going, if Democrats get power in 2020, taxes will skyrocket out of your pocket. They represent an existential economic threat to the United States of America.

This does NOT include state, local, excise, gas and property taxes.

Now just think,
"What if Government Stayed the Same Size as in 1959?"

We were a great country of opportunity back then. But slowly over the years, people kept falling for the lie told by Democrats that they would be better off if there was a huge nanny government to take care of them. Over the years our taxes kept going up and up and in the 1970's women had to start entering the workforce in very large numbers to make ends meet. I say this would NOT have been necessary if we rejected the big government big taxes strategy of the Democrat Party.

Now we are in the situation where our total national debt is over $23 Trillion dollars. Republicans are just as much at fault in the national debt too. This monster amount is far larger than our Gross Domestic Product for a year. This is what will kill our wonderful country. We are in debt up past our eyeballs and its interest payments that should be used for infrastructure, better education, science inventing new life changing technologies. Instead we have to pay the interest on the loans we made to spend ourselves silly and under cruel reasons that black people are inferior.

How much better off would everyone be if democrats stopped telling the black community that they cannot "make it" on their own but will always require assistance from the Democrat Party. How condescending can you get, how demeaning to tell people they are too stupid to support themselves and make their own way. Herein lies the real racism. Right here. Selling people on the idea they are inferior and need to be dependent on government.

The Democrats have sold lock, stock and barrel the lie that black people are inferior and must get mountains of money to "help them out of poverty". But they will NOT do one of the few things that would really work. It is what Booker T. Washington said so long ago. The key is getting a very good education. But Democrat politics are tightly aligned with the teacher's unions and always vote against school vouchers. This would allow black students the choice of going to better schools than the rat traps they currently are forced into by politicians. It is my opinion that if school vouchers were made legal back decades ago, we would NOT be having the horrific crime rates we do now in black communities. People would be out working, raising families and enjoying the opportunities this nation holds for all of us.

Our nation would look far more like the country Almighty God intended for us here in America if we citizens stopped looking to live off other taxpayers, understand the Democrats for what they really are, a pack of lustful power seeking Satanic demons, understand what Republicans are, really flawed politicians who at least do love this country and know and support the founding principles of our nation. Republicans just have to stop loving war so much.

The Democrat Party Evil Strategy:

Everyone needs to understand the evil that exists within the Democrat party. They are in no way whatsoever a Godly principled organization that wants to do good for humanity and American citizens. They exhibit all the of behavior both in word and deed that are characteristic of a satanically motivated bunch of criminals.

1. Deny deny deny.
2. Create crises
3. manufacture hoaxes
4. perform constant personal attacks

5. accuse other people of what you are doing
6. slither like a snake with hidden agendas in the deep state

In the book "Rules for Radicals" by communist radical Saul Alinsky, you will find the above strategies and how to use them successfully. It is correct to believe that the Democrat party knows full well all of these radical tactics and uses them constantly at all levels of government and interpersonal relationships in order to achieve whatever they wish at whatever cost is borne by other people.

Rules for Radicals, The Democrat Party Playbook:

Saul Alinsky was a 1960s variety communist radical who lived in the United States. He wrote the book called, "Rules for Radicals". It is basically an instruction manual for how to be a communist or socialist radical and gain political power through the use of various dishonest means. It is a godless book that exploits many different forms of dishonesty, lies, misrepresentation, manipulation, and how to influence people regardless of whatever you say may or may not be the truth.

In his book, Alinsky treats the truth with contempt in that it is to be used only if it suits your radical power grapping purpose. And Alinsky spends great amounts of time justifying all forms of lies and dishonesty in light of the socialist political power ends that it is trying to accomplish. Alinsky views life as a series of never ending revolutions. He does not call out for just changing the status quo. Rather he wants to completely revolt against the way things are, no matter how they are. In large part Alinsky wants to live in a society that is constantly revolting against itself.

Alinsky is not a stupid man. He is dangerous because built into his book are assumptions about reality that are just plainly not true. **Alinsky dedicates his book to Lucifer**. Yes, unbelievably so.

Lest we forget at least an over the shoulder acknowledgment to the very first radical: from all our legends, mythology, and history (and to who is to know where mythology leaves off in history begins-or which is which), the first radical known to man who rebuild against the establishment and did it so effectively that he at least won his own kingdom – Lucifer [42]

Saul Alinsky

---

[42] Rules for Radicals, Saul Alinsky, Vintage Books, 1971

I hope this gives you a very good hint as to the evil source of what Saul Alinsky was thinking and promoting in his book. Simply put, everything that Alinsky said was inspired directly by Satan and his admiration of him.

For any Christian this should be enough to reject out of hand everything this man has to say. For any Christian this should be enough to reject anyone or any organization that behaves in accordance with the book, "Rules for Radicals".

As we will now see, it is the Democrat party and its leadership that has chosen to use the filthy tactics that are contained in this Satan inspired book. This alone should be enough to never believe one damned word that the Democrat party has to say.

The Means to an End:

Here are some basic foundational beliefs of Saul Alinsky:

1. "Rules for Radicals is written for the Have-Nots on how to take it away." [43] (from the Haves). Everything Alinsky wrote is geared against anyone considered to have wealth.

2. "In this book we are concerned with how to create mass organizations to seize power and give it to the people." [44]. This last part about giving it to people is just part of the sales pitch.

3. Dogma (Christianity) is the enemy of human freedom. Dogma must be watched for and apprehended at every turn and twist of the revolutionary movement. In other words, throw God out of the picture. To Alinsky, God is in the way of human freedom. BS.

4. We live with a Judeo Christian ethic that has not only accommodated itself to but justified slavery, war, and every other human exploitation of which ever status quo happened to prevail. Alinsky has a terribly perverted hateful view of Christianity.

---

[43] IBID
[44] IBID

5. One man's positive is another man's negative. In other words, if you have something that means someone else does not. That is not equal and very bad. Never mind if you earned it.

6. Mankind is divided into three parts: The Haves, The Have-Nots and the Have-a-Little, Want More. To Alinsky, everything has to do with material possessions and power. He addresses nothing else like morality.

7. The spiritual life of the haves is a ritualistic justification of their possessions.

8. Life is a corrupting process.

9. Everything is relative, there are no absolutes.

10. The ethics of the means to an end is justified by the end. Morality is a fluid concept depending on what the end is.

The above 10 points give is a very good overview regarding the philosophy of life that Saul Alinsky holds true. I cannot find much at all that is in common with the Judeo-Christian principles that our country was founded upon. Alinsky has a very defective foundational understanding of objective reality as created by Almighty God. It is right at the very starting gate of existential philosophy that Saul Alinsky falls on his nose.

People cannot be divided based on possessions. Yet this is a major tenant of Alinsky's worldview. He says power will be given to the people yet never in the history of socialism or communism is power ever yielded to the people. It by definition is always concentrated in the hands of a few exceedingly corrupt yet politically powerful people. His view of Christianity is completely warped and twisted into something unrecognizable by this Christian pastoral minister. Christianity does not justify slavery, war and all the other hateful things Alinsky accuses Christianity of. Again this is a complete distortion and complete lack of understanding on his part. One man's positive is NOT another man's negative. Objective reality as designed by Almighty God has never worked this way and never will. Life does not corrupt in and of itself. Rather it is designed to educate God's children regarding the laws of God and how to love others as you love yourself. Everything is NOT relative. There are absolutes in this physical reality as there are in the spiritual realm. Love God first. That is an absolute. Love others as you love yourself. That too is an absolute. Morality is NOT a fluid concept that changes with circumstances. Some things are just plain wrong and others just plain morally right. Alinsky spends much time in his book demonstrating his total ignorance about these philosophical concepts.

The Rules for Radicals:

1. A person's concern with the ethics of means and ends varies inversely with one's personal interest in the issue
2. The judgment of ethics is dependent upon the political position of those sitting in judgment
3. In war the end justifies almost any means
4. The ethics of means and ends is that judgment must be made in the context of the times in which the action occurred and not from any other chronological vantage point
5. The concern with ethics increases with the number of means available and vice versa
6. The less important the end to be desired is, the more one can afford to engage in ethical evaluations of the means
7. Generally speaking, success or failure is a mighty determinant of ethics.
8. The morality of a means depends upon whether the means is being employed at a time of eminent feet or eminent victory
9. Any effective means is automatically judged by the opposition as being unethical
10. You do what you can with what you have and then close it with moral garments
11. Goals must be phrased in general terms like liberty, equality, fraternity, pursuit of happiness and so on.

The above 11 rules are what radicals of today use against what they call "the status quo". In reading Alinsky's book I never found the word "love". This is highly significant. Of course, I would never expect to see this word in a document that was inspired by Satan and dedicated to the memory of Lucifer. Yet there are many, many radical liberals living in the United States today that are attempting to use the above rules in such a way as to topple our Judeo Christian-based democratic republic.

As of today, the radical leftists known as the Democrat party is actively engaged in using the above godless rules in their continual attempt to gain political power over the American people. Looking at the following rules for political power tactics we can see these tactics and action by the Democrat party in our 2020 election cycle going on right now.

For example, rule number eight says to always keep the pressure on your enemy. Rule number 13 says to pick your target and polarize it. It is these two rules the Democrat party follows when they constantly attack Pres. Trump every day of the week and blame him for everything under the sun whether or not it makes sense to do so. Recently there have been to mass shootings in the United States. One in El Paso Texas and the other one in Dayton Ohio. In both cases Democrats hit the airwaves and blamed Pres. Trump for both tragedies. You will never hear anything positive about President Trump from the Democrats. This would go against their rules for radicals.

They also blame our second amendment and the NRA. Never mind that this attack makes no sense. But they are adhering to rule number eight when they do such idiotic things like this.

The more you understand Saul Alinsky's book, Rules for Radicals, the more you see just how closely the strategies and tactics of the Democrat party follow this Satan inspired book of hate and lust for political power. It is my belief that this is the Democrat party playbook that they are following in our election.

Rules for Political Power Tactics:
To Alinsky, tactics are doing whatever you can with whatever you have at the time.

1. Power is not only what you have but what the enemy thinks you have. Notice the warlike terminology. He views other people as "the enemy."
2. Never go outside the experience of the people on your side. In other words use the experience of your people and don't go beyond that
3. whenever possible, do go outside of the experience of the enemy.
4. Make the enemy live up to their own book of rules. In other words, use morality, ethics and other such items against your enemy while you are free to ignore all of that.
5. Ridicule your enemy whenever possible. It is almost impossible to counterattack ridicule.
6. A good tactic is one that your people enjoy doing.
7. A tactic that drags on too long becomes a drag
8. Always keep the pressure on your enemy. Never let them rest.
9. The threat of a tactic is usually more terrifying than the tactic itself.
10. The major premise or tactics is the development of operations that will maintain a constant pressure on the opposition.
11. If you push a negative hard and deep enough, it will break through into its counter side.
12. The price of a successful attack is a constructive alternative.
13. Pick the target, freeze it, personalize it and then polarize it. In other words, do not attack organizations. Rather attack individuals that can be isolated as a

specific target. A target must be a personification. In this way more hostility can be focused.

A personal encounter with three Democrats in front of the Santa Clara City Council.

A number of years ago when my family lived in Santa Clara California we had a serious problem every weekend. Approximately ½ mile from our neighborhood was a gay bar called "The Tinkers Damn". It was obviously a meeting place for gay people to meet up and then do whatever they do. The problem was that the customers of The Tinkers Damn discovered the cul-de-sac that my family and others with children lived in.

They would at night drive a car into our eight house cul-de-sac, park there and do whatever they do. Then they would throw the used condoms out the window for the homeowners to clean up after them. These perverts did not care one bit about the danger they willfully and purposely posed to all the young children that lived there. In total there were 10 small children that lived in our eight home cul-de-sac. But each Saturday morning and each Sunday morning I would personally find gooey and slimy used condoms on the sidewalk or on the curb and sometimes in the shrubbery. My children were between the ages of seven and thirteen. Other families also found these wretched diseased laden condoms in front of their homes too. We all learned we needed to go on "condom patrol" each weekend morning to protect our children before they went out to play.

We complained to the city and nothing was done. We finally made a formal proposal to wall off the street that gave them access to our quiet neighborhood. This prompted a city Council meeting where many hundreds of people showed up to the point where not everyone could fit inside. The city provided speakers outside of the building so the excess could hear the goings-on.

Now as it was, there was a large apartment complex on an adjacent street that had four streets they could use to come and go. The "apartment people" objected vehemently against the proposal to block that one entry which by the way was cumbersome to use as it went through our neighborhood.

The democrats that led the apartment people accused us homeowners of being terrible people. Here is a list of the accusations they threw at us during the city council meeting:

1.   Our position was a conspiracy against the apartment people

2. The objective of our conspiracy was to drive up property values at the expense of the apartment people. Now, how in the hell that could be is beyond any form of reason.

3. They said that, get this, people who lived in the apartments would DIE because emergency vehicles could not get to victims in time. Totally a lie as our streets are completely out of the way. This is why the homosexuals chose to do their business in our area.

4. We were mean and cruel against the apartment people

5. They accused us of feeling superior above them

The list of wretched comments went on and on not making any kind of sense. You had to be there but their tone of voice, their finger pointing etc was an awful sight to see.

This story is but one small example of the mindset that Democrats have against people who do not agree with them. This is a real life story. This really did happen as explained above. I want you to notice that the above things that the Democrat people said are highly consistent with how the Democrat party works. They have a very consistent hostile mindset against anybody that is different from them and thinks differently. Yet it is the same people who accuse others of precisely what they do.

I have said it before, and I will say it again. This is fully consistent with the strategies and tactics of Satan on this earth. He wants to divide people and set them against each other in order to let that lead to their destruction. This is precisely what happened at the Santa Clara city Council meeting that evening. I find the liberal Democrat mindset to be a disgusting morass of sinful and hateful thoughts that guide sinful and hateful actions against others of God's children.

Remember: All of us God's children are fighting against forces and principalities in the spirit world. The war takes place in the minds of men.

Ephesians 6:12, For our struggle is not against flesh and blood, but against the rulers, against the authorities, against the powers of this dark world and against the spiritual forces of evil in the heavenly realms.

Satan is the prince of this earth until he is cast into eternal hell which has not happened yet. From what we see all around us is that Satan is alive and well in the minds of the Democrat party, especially the leaders.

On that evening in Santa Clara at the Council Satan was obviously in the minds of the people who were throwing such terrible accusations against us homeowners who only wanted to protect our children from the dangers of used dripping wet condoms. Nobody wants to clean up used condoms off the sidewalk in front of their house. But, for wanting to provide a safe environment for our children we were castigated by the Democrat representatives, we were accused mercilessly of being wretched cruel and mean-spirited people who wanted apartment dwellers to die if there was an emergency.

Take this one example my dear children of God, learn from it and start observing the pattern of this one incident that exists throughout our entire national political system through the words and actions of the Democrat party.

The Third Democrat Debate, September 12, 2019:

I saw the third Democrat debate today on September 12, 2019. The field has been whittled down to 10 contestants. I want to put this small discussion within the section about the 10 Commandments because, **boy did they ever violate the Commandments in saying what they did** and how they said it to the American people and to each other. Here are a few observations that I saw this evening.

1. This whole thing was to be considered nothing more than verbal warfare based on individual style and who they picked on for their target. Bernie Sanders attacked ABC for the sin of partnering with the healthcare industry. We all must remember that Bernie Sanders is a communist, a 100% complete communist, and he will attack any free enterprise and free market corporation that provides goods and services at remarkably low cost to the entire population of the United States. Bernie is demented enough to actually believe companies are evil. This was just a mindless attack in an effort to assassinate whatever credibility ABC may have in the political arena. Did you know that Jesus Christ considers attacking a person's reputation is tantamount to murder? There are specific reasons for this based in biblical times.

When you listen to politicians always pay serious and close attention to their body language. It is very revealing about the kind of person they really are. Books are written on this topic. Read one. It is illuminating.

Bernie's index finger got a real work out during the debate as well. It seems Bernie is unable to speak without pointing his index finger at people in a very demeaning manner. Psychologically this is very revealing because it shows a person who honestly believes they are far better than anyone else, have dominion over other "lesser people" and their finger-pointing action proves this because

Bernie loves to lecture people about how terrible they are. It is Bernie who is terrible. **He should look in the mirror one day and lecture himself.** Now there is a very frightening experience that he would probably never recover from. Do you realize that if Bernie had a white background behind him, he would look bald? Just a thought.

Also, tone of voice is ever so important. Did anyone notice how they yelled at each other. This shows a lack of respect for their fellow Democrats. Again, it also shows that each of them feel they are "better people" than all the others. Bernie is the poster boy for this demeaning behavior.

2. The whole evening was sickening to me because when you boil it all down all 10 of these contestants were arguing over just a few things.

    a. How should they confiscate more money from American taxpayers and give it to other people that have not earned it, have not spent any of their productive life in creating the wealth, are many times illegally in the country but Democrats feel they in some mysterious way deserve the products and wealth created by the productive lives of others of God's children. Said simply the Democrats were arguing with each other how many goodies they are going to give to the have-nots from those who have created the wealth.

    This is a total violation of the 10th Commandment where the Democrats covet and envy the wealth produced by the sacrifices and work of the taxpaying God's children in our country. These people are taken for granted and are ignored by the Democrat party except for their wealth which the Democrats want to confiscate from them and feel virtuous in doing so. Frankly the Democrats are on a freeway to hell with no speed limit.

    b. The big issue of the night was how do they want to fleece the American people and fool them into accepting total government control over their health care programs. A rule from "Rules for Radicals" by communist Saul Alinsky is that if you control health care, you control the entire population. This is the Democrat handbook for how to seize political power. All of them are some kind of Socialist/Communist on the stage of the debate. This violates the second of the two great commandments. "Love others, love your neighbor as you love yourself".

REMEMBER, LOVE IS THE GLUE THAT HOLDS THE UNIVERSE TOGETHER.

Democrats have no love for average citizens. This is a terrible but TRUE statement. Remember, politicians get filthy rich by being in office. All of this money must have to come from illegal sources considering the salary they make while in office.

This violates multiple of the 10 Commandments. In my view it violates "thou shalt not steal". They have stolen money from the people through hidden and nefarious deals that have increased their wealth enormously. They have violated the commandment of "thou shalt not lie". They never talk about their wealth therefore it is a lie of omission and when asked about this they have dodged or ignored the subject which is a lie of commission.

In the case of Nancy Pelosi, she lives in San Francisco which is infested with all sorts of pain and agony suffering and death due to homelessness. She has not spoken one word to my knowledge about this problem. Ignoring a problem like this is a violation of thou shalt not lie again. It is a lie of omission, ignoring a horrible human problem that she has been hired along with other Democrats to fix. The real problem is that, it is the Democrats that are the cause of the problem due to their heinous and Satanic political ideology.

I think there should be an 11th commandment which states: thou shalt not be buddies with Satan. This applies to the entire Democratic Party.

c. They argued amongst themselves regarding who had the best plan for healthcare as measured by gargantuan expenditures for the benefit of so many people who were never covered before and worst of all every illegal alien that has successfully crossed our borders without being caught. Do you realize that this includes the 10,000 plus members of the MS 13 gang of thugs YOU PAY FOR MD 13'S HEALTH CARE? But you will never hear this fact from the Democrats. Also, Nancy Pelosi considers these murderous thugs "children of God with a divine spark in their hearts". Sure Nancy, sure, we can see that in the picture.

d.   This discussion certainly violates the Commandments against stealing and also the commandment against envying and coveting your neighbor's goods. The discussion was simply how to plot against taxpaying God's children to confiscate what they have to pay for what they want to give away for free to other people that are more likely to vote for them. This evening however it seems as if they had a harder time trying to appear virtuous and planning these confiscations against God's children.

Again, this is a bunch of greedy and envious socialists arguing over the money and wealth created by the taxpaying God's children in the United States. These characters, these socialist creatures of the swamp actually act as if the money is there's. I say it again. IT IS NOT! But these reptilian's with serious brain dysfunctions actually believe they have a complete right and duty to strip the wealth and income of the taxpaying public and give it free to those people that the Democrats feel will be most likely to vote for them if they give that money away.

I like to watch Westerns on television. There was an episode where five crooks were deciding how to split the loot that they rob from a stagecoach. This is precisely what the Democrats were doing at their disgusting debate this evening. They did not talk about splitting the loot in obvious terms because they ignored completely that aspect of spending other people's money. They simply ignored the fact that their plan was to confiscate trillions of dollars from people who traded their sacred life in the form of work for the benefit of themselves and their families health and well-being. The victims of these socialist snake like creatures did not see this coming against them. But I do and I write about it. I vowed to God that I will always pursue the truth no matter where it takes me. And right now I have to say covering the Democrat reptilian's really puts a strain on my nervous system and my sense of Judeo-Christian justice and our loving principles to love God and to love our neighbors as ourselves. These are the two great commandments as Jesus has told us. Yet I could find no evidence whatsoever of these two great commandments in the debates the Democrat reptiles had this evening.

They characterize these programs as evidence of how good and nice these creatures are and how loving they are. This is one big fat ass lie. And as such it certainly violates the commandment against lying. And they lied both popular ways. They lied by stating falsehoods of commission where they purposely said things that were not true. They lied by omission because they never mentioned the disaster, the economic disaster that they would be perpetrating on the American people and all the resulting pain, suffering and death that will result as it has 100% of the time in human history for anything like the socialism they are proposing. To think that grown adults would behave this way is so sad and so mind-boggling it makes me want to puke on Joe Biden's shoes.

3. The Democrats biggest lie of omission was centered around the total silence they treated our rip roaring economy in United States right now. By many objective economic measures, our country is doing far better than it ever has. One of my favorite statistics shows that both Latino unemployment and black unemployment are at all-time lows. This is wonderful and the gap of earned wages between Blacks, whites and Latinos has shrunk to gather to all-time lows as well. All this is because of this stewardship of the economy by Pres. Donald Trump. The stock market has doubled since he was elected as another point of information. But the Democrats at their debate never mentioned any of this. This was a perfect time for them to inform the American public about the condition of our country and how they could make it even better. Instead, they bickered between themselves on how to give away other people's money, ignored the great condition of our economy today and tried to give economic credit to Barack Obama which is one of the most asinine moments of the evening.

4. It was a sickening display of politics by association when Joe Biden kept saying the putrid phrase "I am with Barack". The man doesn't have any real good ideas by himself, so he tries to bask in the putrid glow of the Muslim communist named Barack Obama.

Summary: the socialist/communist Democrat party debate this evening on September 12, 2019 was a sickening display reptilian creatures doing the best they can to show how wonderful and loving they are by confiscating other people's money in order to give it away for free to those people who these reptilian's feel will vote for them. In essence this is how these creatures spent three hours on national television. The manners in which they all tried to do virtue signaling whereby each of them tried to demonstrate how much of a wonderful caring loving and giving person they are was enough to send anybody to the medicine cabinet for anti-nausea medicine which I do have an I did use.

The Democrat party of 2020 will most certainly destroy our constitutional republic and our free market democracy all the while they are thinking how virtuous and wonderful they are while completely ignoring the truth of socialism and communism and the hundreds of millions of people that have died since Carl Marx first wrote the Communist manifesto in the early 20th century.

Democrat Attacks Against United States Sovereignty:
There are certain key elements that must be present for a country to maintain its sovereignty and international recognition. These elements include the following:

1. represented by one centralized government
2. this centralized government as sovereignty over a specified geographic area
3. a permanent population
4. a defined territory
5. the capacity to enter into relations with other sovereign states
6. each sovereign nation has the right to determine its own political status and exercise permanent sovereignty within the limits of their territorial jurisdiction
7. a Constitution that determines the powers and duties of the sovereign government
8. citizens are given fundamental rights which become overarching limitations to the power of the state and its sovereignty
9. sovereignty is indivisible and cannot be divided into parts

10. in the United States we are unique. It is recognized that it is, "We the People", who are sovereign. It is we the people who hold ultimate sovereignty in this United States. This sovereignty has been bequeathed to us by Almighty God. We in turn lend our sovereignty to the state by means of who we vote for and the laws that we determine to live under. If we the people no longer are satisfied with our government, we have the power to change it. The state does not have ultimate and final authority in the United States, we the people do.

The above represents the key necessities of a sovereign state. It must have the necessary tools in order to govern itself and serve the needs of its citizens. A sovereign country must be able to control who is allowed into the country and what limitations are placed on people who enter. Every country in the world has these rights through its sovereignty. In almost all countries on Earth there are stiff punishments if you enter the country illegally.

The current Democrat party has adopted policies that are aimed directly at destroying the sovereignty of the United States of America.

In other articles and resources that I have researched I have found that the reason Margaret Sanger wanted aggressive birth control was to get rid of Blacks in our country. Apparently, Hillary Clinton likes this idea a lot to her admiration of Sanger. And the Democrat party was so much in love with Hillary Clinton they nominated her to run for president in 2016. What does this tell you about the Democrat party in general regarding their true feelings about racism and other topics? It does not take much thinking to figure this out.

Part Four

The Democrat 2020 Platform

The Democrat 2020 Platform:
Democrats Do the Will of Satan:

No voter ID. Democrats feel strongly that in order to vote a person should never have to identify themselves with a government issued ID. They say that like so many other things, this is racist, xenophobic and hateful against minorities and the poor. Democrats never mention the fact that due to previous negligence on the part of multiple previous presidents not enforcing our immigration laws, we have around 20 million illegal aliens in our country today, possibly millions more. We just do not know.

Without government issue ID, all of these people would have enough political power to select our next president. Think about this. Does any reasonable thinking person in the United States want illegal aliens to have the deciding votes on who will run our federal government in the next four years?

When Valid IDs Are REQUIRED:			When Valid IDs are Not Required:
• Driving	• Transacting with a Bank	• Applying for Section 8 Housing	Voting
• Boarding an Airplane	• Sending a Wire Transfer	• Applying for a H-1B Visa, or Green Card	
• Purchasing a Car	• Applying for Online Banking	• Holding a Rally or Protest	
• Getting a Car Registration	• Applying for Store Credit	• Buying a Firearm	
• Renting a Car / Boat / Jet Ski / etc.	• Establishing a Utilities Account (Water / Light / Electric / Cable / Gas / etc.)	• Adopting a Pet	
• Buying Insurance	• Cashing a Check	• Applying for a Hunting License	
• Buying Train Tickets	• Getting a Credit Card	• Applying for a Fishing License	
• Obtaining a Passport	• Opening a Retirement Account	• Joining a Gym	
• Picking up mail from FedEx, UPS, Post Office, etc.	• Applying for a Mortgage	• Using Pawn Shops	
• Renting Tools / Furniture / Equipment	• Buying a House	• Buying Annual Tickets to Amusement Parks	
• Visiting a Doctor's Office / Hospital	• Applying for Apartment Rentals	• Entering Night Clubs	
• Getting Outpatient Testing	• Renting a Hotel Room	• Volunteering at Non-Profit Organizations	
• Donating Blood	• Buying a Cell Phone	• Voting in a Union Election	
• Getting a Prescription	• Going to Court	• Buying Cigarettes	
• Buying Certain OTC Cold Medications, and products like nail polish remover	• Entering Federal Buildings	• Buying Liquor	
• Applying for a Job	• Getting a Business License	• Visiting a Casino	
• Applying to School	• Getting a State ID	• Buying an "M"-Rated Video Game	
• Applying for a Professional License	• Cashing in a Large Lottery Ticket Win	• Going to Jail	
• Getting Married	• Obtaining Medicare / Medicaid	• Participating in Outdoor Activites Like Sky diving, Bungee Jumping, etc	
• Check Out a Book from the Library	• Applying for Food Stamps	• Participating in Political Events	
• Joining the Military	• Applying for Welfare		
• Adopting a Child	• Applying for Unemployment		
	• Using Social Security Services		

Do You Think People Can Manage to Register for a Voter ID?

The Democrats do! This is because they have promised so much free this and free that to illegal aliens in this country that they will certainly get the illegal vote. Listening to the Democrats is one very good way for this country to commit suicide. And the Democrats will get what they want most in life which is not to serve the American people but to control them through confiscation of their productive well and mountains of rules and regulations that will reach into every facet of human existence. These people want control over God's children not to serve but to control. This is the very same thing that Satan wanted so very very long ago.

Remember, the Democrat party is Satan's political arm in the United States.

No borders. Every country in the United States to must have specified geographic areas. In other words, there must be borders that define the land which makes up the country and separates it from its neighbors. Without this there is no country. This is very plain to see and not arguable. But the Democrat party does not want the United States to have borders anymore.

The Democrat party wants to abolish both our northern and southern borders. They want to allow anyone from anywhere on the planet to freely come here.

Abolish ICE and DHS. Democrats want to completely destroy our means of protecting ourselves from illegal aliens many of whom are criminals, human traffickers, drug dealers and so on. Forget the image of only peaceful families with hard working talented adults coming here as the Democrat commercials portray.

Just take a moment and think about if we abolished ICE, abolished the DHS, opened up our poling places to anyone who came in to vote with no identity. Think about what this country would be like in a short five years.

Here are a few thoughts that come to mind:
1. More and more low class and criminal class people come here
2. Government welfare goes through the roof
3. Government deficits rise terribly
4. Violent crime would skyrocket.
5. Violence in the streets, urban areas and extending into suburbs will climb wildly. This means roving mobs of different sizes wandering around neighborhoods at night doing the crime they do best.

6. People in control of government would be the criminal element. Just look at Chicago and New York and San Francisco

7. Tax revenue would plummet both state and federal, simple economics, millions more illegal aliens arrive, costs for them skyrocket, Democrats in congress increase taxes of all kinds, this causes the economy to tank, always has, unemployment increases greatly, average wages decrease substantially, government deficits increase greatly, interest payments go up along with interest rates that put more brakes on the economy. Violence increases as a war of "the haves" against the "have nots" breaks out all around the country.

8. Investment markets, stocks, collapse due to lack of confidence in government, markets

9. Society will unravel as everyone will be fighting everyone else

All of this happens because of the Democrat Party's lust for control, dominion, over our country. Their "damn everyone" do anything even if it destroys the country political strategy just to get elected to rule over a resulting dung heap with a dominating smile on their faces. This is exactly what will put a smile on Satan's face.

Changing the United States Demographics:

Attack President Trump for everything he does and use the lie or HOAX as grounds for impeachment,

Ukraine foreign minister defends Trump's call with Zelenskiy: 'I think there was no pressure'.

A top Ukrainian official on Saturday defended President Trump's July phone call with Ukranian President Volodymyr Zelenskiy, during which Trump reportedly urged authorities in Kiev to investigate dealings in the Eastern European county by the son of former Vice President Joe Biden.

BIDEN FACES SCRUTINY FOR DEMANDING OUSTER OF UKRAINE OFFICIAL PROBING FIRM THAT EMPLOYED HIS SON

"Now that the Democrats and the Fake News Media have gone 'bust' on every other of their Witch Hunt schemes, they are trying to start one just as ridiculous as the others, call it the Ukraine Witch Hunt, while at the same time trying to protect Sleepy Joe Biden," Trump said. "Will fail again!"

The Fake News Media didn't want to report that "Joe Biden [demanded] that the Ukrainian Government fire a prosecutor who was investigating his son, or they won't get a very large amount of U.S. money," the president had said.

"[So] they fabricate a [...] story about me and a perfectly fine and routine conversation I had with the new President of the Ukraine. Nothing was said that was in any way wrong, but Biden's demand, on the other hand, was a complete and total disaster," Trump said.

Headline:
Pelosi announces launch of formal impeachment inquiry into Trump

Speaker Nancy Pelosi (D-Calif.) on Tuesday announced the launch of a formal impeachment inquiry into President Trump.

The move follows sustained pressure from the progressive wing of her party that on Tuesday quickly snowballed to include moderates, liberal holdouts, vulnerable Democrats, committee chairs and party icons.

Remember the Democrats tried to impeach Pres. Trump before he became president back in 2016. Then the Mueller hoax came. And now another impeachment with absolutely zero evidence against the President. This will never stop unless voters stop them and take away all power.

Would you vote for somebody that wants to fire a person for no reason? This is what the Democrats want to do to Pres. Trump because they lost an election. Anybody who votes for this type of chaos is voting for the destruction of the United States of America and the complete abandonment of our Judeo-Christian principles, ethics and morality. It is my belief that any Christian that votes Democrat will have to answer to Jesus Christ himself of such a wanton hateful thing to do.

Democrat Party Godless Strategy and Tactics:
The following is a sampling of Democrat Party tactics against the American people. You will find all these tactics right out of "Rules for Radicals" written by the 1960's communist radical Saul Alinsky. Does anyone really want to vote for politicians that use books for radicals as a guide for election strategies and tactics. Remember that during the 2020 election campaign, everything you see from Democrats has been guided by Saul Alinsky where morality, Christian principles and values cannot be found anywhere. They are completely ignored.

1. **Democrats are anti-Christian, anti-God and anti-constitutional**. It is no secret that Democrats are anti-God, anti-Christian and anti-constitutional but people tend to forget it is these hatreds that is the driving force for the evil they perpetrate.

   a. Todd Starnes: Leftists say judge is unfit to serve because of his Christian beliefs [45]

   b. Pennsylvania state Dems slam Republican's prayer as 'offensive,' bigoted [46]

   c. Ohio school scrubs 92-year-old Ten Commandments plaque after atheists complain. [47]

   d. Leftists Celebrate Independence Day by Burning Declaration of Independence, American Flag [48]

   e. Trump's 'Salute to America' Upsets Democrats, Protesters Burn American Flag in Front of White House [49]

   f. **Eph 6:12:** *For our wrestling is not against flesh and blood, but against the principalities, against the powers, against the world-rulers of this darkness, against the spiritual hosts of wickedness in the heavenly places.* [50]

   g. **Our Spiritual Warfare is Against "Principalities"** so says St Paul in Ephesians. Remember that the real war goes on inside the heads of human beings. Democrats have given their souls to Satan in return for a putrid promise of earthly power and dominion over others of God's children. Does anyone want to live under the laws created by amoral creatures referred to as Democrat leaders?

---

[45]   https://www.foxnews.com/opinion/leftists-say-judge-is-unfit-to-serve-because-of-his-christian-beliefs

[46] https://video.foxnews.com/v/6018642692001/#sp=show-clips

[47] https://www.foxnews.com/us/ohio-school-atheist-complain-ten-commandments

[48]   https://www.blabber.buzz/conservative-news/609097-leftists-celebrate-independence-day-by-burning-declaration-of-independence-american-flag-special?utm_source=c-am&utm_medium=c-am-email&utm_term=c-am-GI

[49] https://www.blabber.buzz/conservative-news/609068-trumps-salute-to-america-upsets-democrats-protesters-burn-american-flag-in-front-of-white-house?utm_source=c-am&utm_medium=c-am-email&utm_term=c-am-GI

[50]

http://www.battleinchrist.com/principalities_powers_world_rulers_of_darkness_spiritual_wickedness_in_spiritual_warfare.htm

Summary: Democrats again and again demonstrate a hatred of everything American and have rejected Almighty God. This is EXACTLY WHAT LUICIFER DID. He is now is the "prince of this earth", condemned to HELL while constantly trying to destroy every one of God's children. That's you and me and our country.

2. **Scapegoating:** Blame President Trump for everything even if it makes no sense. This too is a Satanic Alinsky tactic right out of "Rules for Radicals" as well.

   a. Democrats blamed Trump for both the Dayton, Ohio and El Paso Tx mass shootings

   b. Democrat California governor Gavin Newsom blames the state of Texas for the homeless crisis in San Francisco. He says many of the homeless are from Texas. Newsom was the mayor of San Francisco for years before becoming governor. This scapegoating has achieved new heights in hypocrisy. Though San Francisco has more billionaires per capita than anywhere else in the world, its homeless problem has rivaled third-world nations. [51]

   c. Democrats invent false immigration stories blaming Trump for separating children from adults. Obama started this years ago for good reasons. 30% of children are NOT children of the adults they are with. Rampant fraud at the border.

   d. Democrat Bernie Sanders always blames the top 1% of wage earners for everything. [52] They are the problem he says. Sanders purposely and willfully ignores the truth that the top 10% of wage earners pay 70% of all the taxes. Sanders hates truth when it interferes with his communist manifesto of lies and deceit. This man is Satanic in my opinion. All the signs are there.

   e. Democrat accuses Administration of Torturing Children to Force Border

   on Compromise [53] I ask you, "do you really believe this?" They are saying that those horrific Republicans are purposely using the illegal

---

[51] https://www.foxnews.com/media/gov-gavin-newsom-responsible-homeless-crisis Fox News August 21, 2019.

[52] https://www.youtube.com/watch?v=CHC9UKvrP2M

[53] https://www.newsmax.com/newsfront/karen-bass-border-security-child-separation-asylum-abuse/2019/06/25/id/921967/

alien children as a bargaining chip with the Democrats. This is pure evil.

f. Democrats blame Trump for illegal alien deaths at the southern border. Never mind that during the Obama administration many terrible deaths took place then too. Its just that they ignored these deaths then as it would make Obama look bad. [54]

g. Democrat Sen. Baldwin: Inhumane Trump Administration Is Neglecting Children at the border. False! [55] President Trump is bound to follow the laws enacted by Barry Soweto aka. Barack Hussain Obama. Democrats NEVER complained when Obama enacted these policies but now that Trump is president, they vilify him.

h. Democrat MSNBC's Joy Reid: Trump supporters 'want to see cruelty' toward migrant children [56] This is disgusting to demonize some people because you disagree with them. Again, this is gutter sludge pouring out of the mouth of Joy Reid. Shame! This is again completely consistent with "Rules for Radicals".

i. Democrats Blame Trump for Border Deaths, Accuse Administration of Deliberately "Punishing" Kids to Make a Point. Again, the situation is the same as when Obama was president but no complaints from Democrats then. Hypocrisy.

Summary: It is the act of a dishonest coward to always blame others for what they may have failed at doing. To Democrats the people who disagree with them become a kind of villainous enemy to them. This is an adolescent mindset kind of action. This mindset also violates the second of the two great commandments…love others as you love yourself. Does anyone really want adolescents governing our country?

3. Invent monster hoaxes.

a. The false lie of the Russian collusion now proved to be a colossal LIE. In the end, both Clintons will be in orange jump suits with fashionable silver bracelets. Notice how suddenly nobody is talking about this.

[54] https://www.breitbart.com/border/2019/06/26/20-times-breitbart-reported-migrant-deaths-during-obama-biden-years-and-no-one-cared/

[55] https://www.breitbart.com/clips/2019/06/26/dem-sen-baldwin-inhumane-trump-administration-is-neglecting-children/

[56] MSNBC's Joy Reid: Trump supporters 'want to see cruelty' toward migrant children

However, justice takes time and the willingness of law enforcement to pursue justice.

It is my belief that if William Barr our new honest attorney general does pursue the people who designed and implemented this monster hoax against Donald Trump and the American people, we will see a flurry of arrests, scandals exposed and trials before the 2020 elections. If my instincts are correct, we will find deep connections with the Russian collusion hoax between high ranking officers of our Department of Justice like William Holder, Jim Comey, members of the Democrat National Committee, Hillary Clinton, Bill Clinton, Barack Obama yes, Obama, Loretta Lynch and other high ranking Democrat administration officials. Remember this. All the people involved with this hoax WERE APPOINTED BY BARACK OBAMA.

Everyone needs to give this hoax some serious thought. In essence, the Democrat party attempted to STEAL THE 2016 ELECTION WITH THIS HOAX THEN AFTER TRUMP WAS ELECTED, WE ALL HEARD THE CONSTANT DRUMBEAT OF IMPEACHMENT AGAINST HIM. This amounts to a coup against the president of the United States. Think what our country would be like if these monsters succeeded. We would never be the same again. This is outright treason against our United States. There should be criminal charges brought and prison time for those involved. They tried to destroy the very fabric of our government and country in a lustful lunge toward seizing political power away from the American people.

It is now shown in the daylight that all of this HOAX was a fabricated dossier invented by ex-British spy Christopher Steele and PAID BY HILLARY CLINTON through a company called Fusion GPS. Satan is very pissed that they failed.
Stay tuned.

The climate change hoax. This horrific hoax against the American people deserves a section all its own. This ugly monster is an octopus of lies with it many tentacles spread throughout the DOJ, CIA, and executive branch of our government. It all started in the Obama administration with its subsequent actions against every American citizen in our country. Using climate as a false Democrat invented premise, the Obama administration involved many people to move our country toward a far larger federal government with draconian restrictions on all of God's children who live in the United States. Obama once said proudly that his administration had no scandals. Well, that is BS. All of the scandals have just not been investigated yet. Now they are under William Barr our new attorney general.

Fundamentally the hoax goes like this. For a number of decades now liberals and people placed into certain positions by liberal Democrat administrations have been maintaining that the earth is warming disastrously due to man-made carbon dioxide and methane. They have trotted out many different so-called "scientific" studies that claim to prove that the earth is headed for a worldwide disaster that will wipe out the human race. They further go on to say that this excess carbon dioxide is caused by human generated emissions.

Therefore, we need to take draconian measures in order to avoid this coming catastrophe that will kill all life on earth. Over the last few decades liberals have proposed many awful anti-human measures in order to "reverse the damage to earth that human beings have caused".

Radical liberals have also been saying that due to higher temperatures (not true) there have been a huge increase in forest fires. This is completely false. They want you to believe that the whole world is burning…a lie.

Headline: *Don't believe the hype – fires globally have actually declined 25% since 2003.* [57] *"In reality, there was a whopping 25 percent decrease in the area burned from 2003 to 2019, according to NASA."*

---

[57] https://www.thedailysheeple.com/dont-believe-the-hype-fires-globally-have-actually-declined-25-since-2003/

Global Burned Area (normalized)

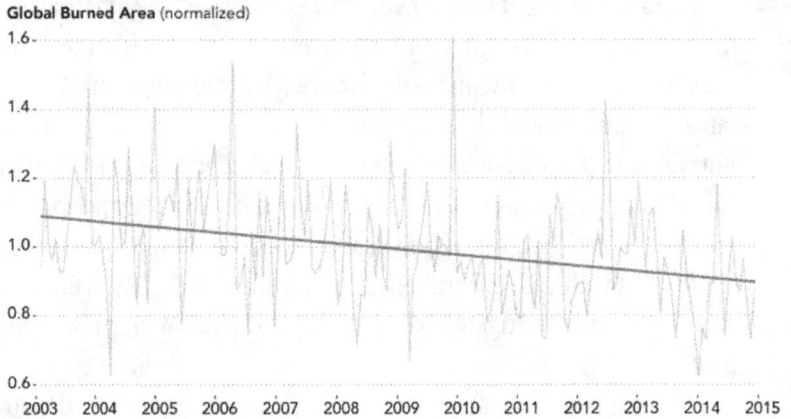

b. Real scientific information about climate, not hoax assertions: [58]
    i.   The climate as always been changing in earth's history…ALWAYS
    ii. Temperature increases in the past are for certain NOT CAUSED BY HUMANS. See appendix A for a detailed history of temperatures
    iii. The Artic and Antarctic are doing better than ever. To say different is a lie.
    iv. Polar Bears are NOT dying but flourishing
    v.   Carbon dioxide is NOT a temperature control substance. Usually temperature increases occur before increases in carbon dioxide. A scientifically correct empirical observation.

Real life mass murder because of the global warming HOAX: In Europe governments have gone completely insane with this global warming idiocy. In Europe, people are dying because they've been told that their sacrifices will save the planet.
    a. European environmentalists hate air conditioners. The European elites openly sneer at America with all our air conditioners. Result: Only 3% of German houses have air conditioners. 2% in India, 3% in the UK, 5% in France.

---

[58] https://www.zerohedge.com/news/2019-09-05/5-surprising-scientific-facts-about-earths-climate

b. Result: In the 2003 heatwave 70,000 people died in Europe because of the summer heat. In 2003 2,000 Brits died, 15,000 died in France, *France24, the country's state-owned television network, advised people suffering from temperatures rising as high as 110 degrees to take cold showers and stick their feet in saucepans of cold water.*7,000 in Germany. *Temperatures in Dusseldorf hit 105 degrees. Officials in Dusseldorf had recently rejected proposals to install air conditioning systems because they're bad for the environment.* [59]

If environmentalists ruled the world according to the climate change HOAX just think how many people would die each year because of their inexcusably insane ideology that has willfully and purposely been propagated by the Democrat party.

70,000 people died in Europe in one hot summer in 2003. This is far more than Islamic terrorists killed in that same year. So, who or what is more dangerous to human life?

I repeat. Environmentalist in Europe KILLED MORE PEOPLE THAN ISLAMIC TERRORISTS IN 2003. I believe that European governments are guilty of crimes against humanity.

c. 90% of American houses have air conditioning. 86% in South Korea, 82% in Australia. People did not die in these countries due to a hot summer. In New York that same year, people put up with the heat and went on with their lives.

Democrats are so insane that they think cows are now a fatal threat to our planet. This is what they think cows look like and what they do. So, this is what Democrats want to do to all of our livestock.

Al Gore, poster boy meadow muffin/cow pie of global warming, now repositioned as climate change predicted New York would be under 20 feet of water by 1988. Gore has made millions scaring people with his "Chicken Little" pronouncements about the world ending. None of it was or is true. I believe he know it also. Satan will shake his

---

[59]   https://www.zerohedge.com/health/have-environmentalists-killed-more-europeans-islamic-terrorists-did

hand when he goes to hell for all the lies he has told the American people in the effort to manipulate us based on this hoax. A large effort was conducted to instill fear into people about mankind destroying the environment to the point we are killing ourselves. According to reliable sources, Gore's house is so large that it consumes 25 times the energy as a normal three bedroom two bath home the rest of us can barely afford. The amount of dung that gets spewed out of this man's mouth should be reason enough to call in emergency EPA people to clean up the mess.

The evil manipulated scientific data: Are the global alarmists right? NO! Are these politicians in any way correct? NO! They used manufactured data and slanted their climate models to produce the result the politicians wanted. [60] The objective truth is that in the past 400 years of measuring global temperatures, the temperature has only increased 3/4 of one degree. [61] [62] This is well within what mother nature does all the time. On a related note did you know that at one time in the history of the earth, our entire planet was covered in ice? Look this up. What caused all the ice to melt? Not mankind. Our climate on earth is constantly and slowly changing. It what our planet does.

The Truth: Climate alarmists have willfully and purposely promoted the use of known faulty computer models that have been programmed to overestimate the global warming hoax. This gives Democrats and others a sense of legitimacy to say that it is scientific to declare human beings are the cause of global warming. The Satanic evil perpetrated here is hidden deep in the computer code or programming of climate models. To those people who think science is God, this is irrefutable evidence. NO!

[60] https://www.zerohedge.com/news/2019-08-12/global-warming-really-existential-threat
[61] http://www.freerepublic.com/focus/f-news/987465/posts
[62] https://www.youtube.com/watch?v=fA5sGtj7QKQ

Part of this HOAX is the pressure put on NASA and NOAA to continue using known faulty computer models that purposely overestimate what is happening. Now finally on September 3, 2019, a truth filled article has been published.

Headline: NASA admits that climate change occurs because of changes in Earth's solar orbit, and NOT because of SUVs and fossil fuels. [63]

(Natural News) For more than 60 years, the National Aeronautics and Space Administration (NASA) has known that the changes occurring to planetary weather patterns are completely natural and normal. But the space agency, for whatever reason, has chosen to let the man-made global warming hoax persist and spread, to the detriment of human freedom.

It was the year 1958, to be precise, when NASA first observed that changes in the solar orbit of the earth, along with alterations to the earth's axial tilt, are both responsible for what climate scientists today have dubbed as "warming" (or "cooling," depending on their agenda). In no way, shape, or form are humans warming or cooling the planet by driving SUVs or eating beef, in other words.

Headline: The Climate Change Alarmists are WRONG, NASA just declared carbon dioxide is GREENING the Earth, NOT killing it. [64]

We show a persistent and widespread increase of growing season integrated LAI (greening) over 25% to 50% of the global vegetated area... Factorial simulations with multiple global ecosystem models suggest that CO2 fertilization effects explain 70% of the observed greening trend...

---

[63] https://dcdirtylaundry.com/nasa-admits-that-climate-change-occurs-because-of-changes-in-earths-solar-orbit-and-not-because-of-suvs-and-fossil-fuels/

[64] https://dcdirtylaundry.com/sorry-climate-change-alarmists-nasa-just-declared-carbon-dioxide-is-greening-the-earth-not-killing-it/

Plants need CO_2 in order to grow and propagate themselves and produce food. All of us learned this in high school. But apparently some people did not and would wind up as Democrats.

For the longest time now, I have been telling people that it is our beloved sun and changes in earth's orbit around it and the slow wobble of the axis of rotation of the earth that is the root cause of change climate. I worked for NASA in the planetary branch right after getting my Bachelor's degree in Chemistry and Physics. I know these things and I know how you can fudge scientific results if you have an evil mind to do so.

This entire hoax is based upon computer models that for decades have projected dramatic warming of the earth by small fossil fueled engines that have produced an incredibly thriving economy and the resulting healthier and longer lives for our citizens. The Democrats want to get rid of all of this in the name of a few degrees centigrade increase in temperature. The consequential death toll from doing this would be beyond anything nuclear war could produce. But the Democrats do not care about human beings.

This climate HOAX is easy to understand. First remember Democrats lust for political power so as to achieve dominion over all the people. This is the very same thing Satan lusted for against God. DOMINION! Rules for Radicals says to never let a crisis go to waste. In this case they are inventing a crisis. Democrats cure for the fake political motivated crisis is to spend $93 TRILLION dollars on a vast central government bureaucracy to control every aspect of human life…in the name of "saving earth". BULLSHOOTY!!! This will shatter any freedoms we have left today as God's children.

Democrats are so closely aligned with Satan that they do not care what the resulting death toll would be on innocent people created by Almighty God. Democrats will say anything and do anything against anybody in order to seize political power. It just so happens that this is the same goal that Satan had when he rebelled against Almighty God. Although he is still Prince of this planet he is condemned to hell for all eternity. Through the grace of God, he is just not there yet and is still able to attack all of God's children which he is currently doing through the Democrat party.

Back to the science of things. All these computer models used by the United Nations have constantly and completely overestimated the temperature increases from the small amount of increase of carbon dioxide. They have overestimated not by a little but by a great amount to the point where these computer models can be never believed because their projections do not come close to real measurements made on the earth.

Atmospheric scientist John Christy from NASA *"compared the average model projections since 1979 to the most reliable observations — those made by satellites and weather balloons over the vast tropics. The result? In the upper levels of the lower atmosphere, **the models predicted seven times as much warming as has been observed. Overprediction also occurred at all other levels.** Christy recently concluded that, on average, the projected heating by the models is three times what has been observed."* [65]

We have all heard in the past decades the scaremongering from the Democrats about climate change or global warming. They knowingly used the false results of these computer models for their political purposes. They described this as a crisis that will kill all of us.

Now, remember what Saul Alinsky said in his book "Rules for Radicals". He said never let a crisis go to waste. This manufactured crisis was being used by the Democrat party to justify so many terrible policies they wanted to put in action against the American people and increase the power of a centralized government over every aspect of the lives of our citizens. The Democrat lust for power knows no limits and

[65] https://www.zerohedge.com/news/2019-08-26/great-failure-climate-models

again they will say anything and do anything in order to satisfy their satanic lust for political power. This is what they have done with this monster claimant change global warming hoax against us all.

Here below are some of the antics that Democrats have been involved with promoting this monster hoax against the American people.

a. Gov. Jay Inslee: As President I Can Stop the Influx of Migrants by Solving Climate Crisis. This bozo clown actually thinks illegal aliens are coming here because the earth warmed up ¾ a degree in the past 400 years. What a monster hoax. Just how stupid does he think we are? [66] Just how stupid is Jay? This cartoon politician actually believes that people are willing to risk their lives on the 2,000 mile trek to the United States because Nicaragua, Honduras and so on has warmed up less than one degree. The word moron just scratches the surface as far as this Democrat goes. He will drop out of the presidential race very soon.

b. House Democrats Spread 'Lies' About Climate Change and Hurricanes, Scientist Says. *"Atmospheric scientist Ryan Maue, a hurricane expert, tweeted that the Democrats' hearing "spreads lies" about the scientific consensus on climate change and hurricanes."* [67] *"Not a good look for next House hearing on climate change and disasters that furthers inaccurate information (spreads lies) from Union of Concerned Scientists on hurricanes."* [68]

c. The Green New Deal is another monster HOAX. **This is a hoax based upon a hoax.** Saikat Chakrabarti and Alexandra Ocasio Cortex manufactured the Green New Deal NOT to address climate change. NO! In the beginning they said the green new deal is

---

[66] https://www.breitbart.com/clips/2019/06/25/inslee-as-president-i-can-stop-the-influx-of-migrants-by-solving-climate-crisis/
[67] https://www.thedailysheeple.com/house-democrats-spread-lies-about-climate-change-and-hurricanes-scientist-says/
[68] IBID

desperately needed to solve the global climate change global warming problem. They said if we do not do this within the next 12 years the earth will never recover, and mankind will cease to exist.

They now admit it was to completely destroy the free market democracy in the United States and replace that with a monster large socialist government. They admit they LIED to us with this Green New Deal. It was designed to be a trap against the American people.

d. Democratic 2020 hopeful Sen. Bernie Sanders on Thursday released his plan for a Green New Deal – promising that the $93 trillion multitrillion-dollar plan to radically overhaul the economy and combat climate change will **"pay for itself"** over the next 15 years. "As president, Bernie Sanders will launch the decade of the Green New Deal, a ten-year, nationwide mobilization centered around justice and equity during which climate change will be factored into virtually every area of policy, from immigration to trade to foreign policy and beyond," his campaign said in a press release.

Does anyone really think that this 74 year old communist who loves Fidel Castro, Karl Marx and Joseph Stalin believe that he can predict the economic impact this HOAX will produce? NO! He cannot. Reality does not matter this white hair brained lunatic. But he is willing to take our country down the socialist infected rathole with his delusions along with no knowledge of God's reality as it actually exists. Remember that he took his honeymoon in Moscow meeting with all kinds of communists. This man is seriously mentally ill. Insane. And he wants to run our country. OMG!

What kind of human being is willing to take 320 million people who live in the greatest country ever founded by mankind down a pain filled road of death proven to be a 100% failure in history producing pain, suffering and death to those who tried it? This Green New Deal is a HOAX SOLUTION BASED ON A HOAX PROBLEM. Monster lies. Everything that come out of the mouth of Bernie Sanders is a disaster built on the lies of socialism and the deaths of tens of millions of innocent people socialism has caused in human history. [69]

e. Now, if you still believe that climate change (formerly global warming) is wrecking our planet and you will die if you do not vote Democrat in 2020, then understand the following facts: [70]

    a. Building one wind turbine requires 900 tons of steel, 2,500 tons of concrete and 45 tons of plastic.

    b. "Renewable energy" is a misnomer. Wind and solar machines and batteries are built from nonrenewable materials. And they wear out. Old equipment must be decommissioned, generating millions of tons of waste.

    c. A single electric-car battery weighs about 1,000 pounds. Fabricating one requires digging up, moving and processing more than 500,000 pounds of raw materials somewhere on the planet. The alternative? Use gasoline and extract one-tenth as much total tonnage to deliver the same number of vehicle-miles over the battery's seven-year life.

    d. A wind or solar farm stretching to the horizon can be replaced by a handful of gas-fired turbines, each no bigger than a tractor-trailer.

    e. Last year a Dutch government-sponsored study concluded that the Netherlands' green ambitions alone would consume a major share of global minerals. "Exponential growth in [global] renewable energy production capacity is not possible with present-day technologies and annual metal production," it concluded.

[69] https://www.foxnews.com/politics/sanders-releases-16-trillion-plus-green-new-deal-plan-promises-it-will-pay-for-itself
[70] https://www.wsj.com/articles/if-you-want-renewable-energy-get-ready-to-dig-11565045328

> f. *What's more, mining and fabrication require the consumption of hydrocarbons. Building enough wind turbines to supply half the world's electricity would require nearly two billion tons of coal to produce the concrete and steel, along with two billion barrels of oil to make the composite blades. More than 90% of the world's solar panels are built in Asia on coal-heavy electric grids.*

Remember what Alexandria Ocasio Cortez and her communist buddy Saikat Chakrabarti said: The Green New Deal was never about climate. It is about changing the entire society to socialism. What a pack of God d*amned LIARS!

3. Other Hoaxes:

a. We must impeach Donald Trump as soon as possible. This is the most asinine and ludicrous thought in our country today. I remember hearing one Democrat intellectual guru start calling for the impeachment of Donald Trump a few days after the election. They claimed the election was a hoax. Remember, this kind of statement comes out of the book "rules for radicals" written by communist and radical Saul Alinsky. In the book it says, "always accuse others of what you yourself are doing".

b. I consider this one of the worst hoaxes perpetrated on the American people. The felon is Google. No real surprise there. Google is managed by rabid radical leftists and like all Democrat leaders and politicians, they are not above lying to the American people. The lie is the results on searches for conservative content on the internet.

"Dr. Robert Epstein: Study claims Google reflected 'very dramatic bias' in 2016 election search results." [71] According to Dr. Robert one of the researchers, *"I looked at politically oriented searches that these people were conducting on Google, Bing and Yahoo. I was able to preserve more than 13,000 searches and 98,000 web pages, and I found very dramatic bias in Google's search results... favoring Hillary Clinton -- whom I supported strongly."*

The bottom like is that we now have extremely bigoted, biased radical leftists that do not give a damn about the United States citizens, they hate the truth of

---

[71] https://www.foxnews.com/media/google-bias-search-results-trump-clinton-epstein-levin

things so they pervert it because then can, to hell with morality and fair play, they only want DOMINION over the people they call customers by controlling what they see on-line. This dear reader is a Satanic method of lying and hate against the children of God. Remember, Satan works through people in clever and nefarious ways. Here is one of them.

c. Rosie O'Donnell Claims 'Over 100,000' 'Concentration Camps' in U.S [72] She offer zero proof of this accusation, just more mindless and hateful blather from a radical liberal forked tongue. This is just one example of ever so many outrageous accusations from Democrats.

d. Alexandra Ocasio Cortex: Photos Reveal AOC Was Crying Over an Empty Parking Lot. It was a fabricated photo shoot to show her crying over imprisoned illegal children held apart from adults. 1/3 of the kids are DNA proved NOT to be related to the adult claiming them as their child. The reason for the separation. [73]

e. Toilet Water: Ocasio-Cortez's 'Drinking Out of Toilets' Claim Drastically Falls Apart. Said women were forced to drink water out of a toilet bowl. [74] I ask just what kind of human being does it take to perpetrate such massive

lies to innocent American citizens. The answer is a person who wants political power and dominion over innocent Americans at any cost to "We the People".

f. Imprisoned Children: This was an orchestrated photo shoot to create the image that OAC was crying for imprisoned children at our southern border. It was all FAKE as the pictures show clearly. The pictures were from a parking lot with a police car in the background. Another HOAX.

---

[72] https://www.blabber.buzz/conservative-news/601848-rosie-odonnell-claims-over-100000-concentration-camps-in-us-special

[73] https://www.zerohedge.com/news/2019-06-27/photos-reveal-aoc-was-crying-over-empty-parking-lot

[74] https://www.blabber.buzz/conservative-news/607656-photo-ocasio-cortezs-drinking-out-of-toilets-claim-drastically-falls-apart-special?utm_source=c-alrt&utm_medium=c-alrt-email&utm_term=c-alrt-Yahoo

g. There is an out of control menace of mass shootings in our country because of too many guns and especially assault rifles. Although many people believe this to be true as it is exaggerated from the Democrat party, the cold hard facts are simply that there is no evidence of an epidemic of mass shootings in our country today. This is yet another hoax perpetrated by Democrats who want to kill our second amendment rights and the ability for us to protect ourselves from criminals and especially our own government. [75]

STATISTICALLY YOU ARE MORE LIKELY TO BE KILLED BY HILLARY CLINTON THAN BY AN AR 15. [76]

Think about this in real world terms. Democrats are very good at banding together and singing from the same song book. As this is being written, they all have been pounding the "mass shooting" drum in their continuing effort to convince us that we have become a nation of "mass shooters" all who vote for President Trump. We must drastically restrict "gun rights" so we can prevent more killings. To a person that is ignorant about the facts this seems good. But the facts are completely wrong, and this footnote is the key to objective truth on this topic. [77] This is yet again another lying HOAX willfully and purposely perpetrated by the Democrat party to push gigantic government controls over every aspect of our lives.

h. *Crime-ridden San Francisco has introduced new sanitized language for criminals, getting rid of words such as "offender" and "addict" while changing "convicted felon" to "justice-involved person.* [78] This is just another way to hide the ugly reality of the situation regarding high levels of crime now in San Francisco. This is exactly what Satan does to hide the truth from all people on earth.

i. Headline*: "Rashida Tlaib sued for alleged assault and battery of Laura Loomer. Damages Demanded Are in Excess of $2 Million USD. The complaint further*

---

[75] https://reason.com/podcast/james-alan-fox-there-is-no-evidence-of-an-epidemic-of-mass-shootings/
[76] https://www.freedomwatchusa.org/statistically-you-are-more-likely-to-be-killed-by-hillary-cl
[77] https://www.freedomwatchusa.org/statistically-you-are-more-likely-to-be-killed-by-hillary-cl
[78] https://www.blabber.buzz/conservative-news/641937-san-francisco-board-rebrands-convicted-felon-as-justice-involved-person-sanitizes-other-crime-lingo-special?utm_source=c-alrt&utm_medium=c-alrt-email&utm_term=c-alrt-Yahoo

alleges that Tlaib, a vehement anti-Semite and vowed opponent of Israel's right to exist, assaulted and battered conservative female Jewish journalist Laura Loomer during a campaign event in Minneapolis" Please take note of this woman as she is arrested for assault and battery at a political event. Do YOU really want to live under the laws this kind of woman would force on all of us?

"We have to make the tough, courageous changes that completely transform a political and economic system that is now built for corporations (and profits), not people," Tlaib wrote. *"Choosing the status quo means doing nothing and giving up. We need a political revolution,"*[79] she added in a call reminiscent of Sen. Bernie Sanders' (I-VT) political pleas. This woman does not give a damn how terribly her politics will hurt our children of God. It takes a huge amount of ignorance, hate of America, hate of white people, hate for our constitutional republic and love for Satanic lust for dominion over God's children anyway she can get it. She should be declared an enemy of the state and put in prison in my humble opinion. Do not dismiss her or other Democrats like her. She could very well be the vanguard of their Communist world view to be forced on all of us.

If any person especially Christians vote for even one Democrat in 2020, you have completely lost your mind!
One fine day you will have to explain this to Jesus Christ Himself.
No Jesus is not conservative nor liberal. He loves all God's children.
However, voting to strip His children of their God given rights
is cause for explaining why a Christian would ever
do such a thing against God Himself through His Children.

i.   Headline: *"Psychiatrists willing to breach professional ethics to participate in House Democrats event scrutinize Trump's mental health. "*[80] Democrats are now in the process of inventing another hoax regarding the mental stability of President Trump. Yup. They are putting together a team of psychiatrists that

---

79   https://www.blabber.buzz/conservative-news/653374-tlaib-calls-for-a-political-revolution-and-complete-transformation-of-political-system-special?utm_source=c-pm&utm_medium=c-pm-email&utm_term=c-pm-GI
80   https://www.thedailysheeple.com/psychiatrists-willing-to-breach-professional-ethics-to-participate-in-house-democrats-event-scrutinize-trumps-mental-health/

are willing to completely breach their professional code of ethics and participate in a public evaluation of President Trump's mental health.

This is awful because *"none of the psychiatrists have treated the president and the American Psychiatric Association (APA) prohibits members from speculating about the mental state of public figures."* So, we already know that whoever participates in this character assassination is violating their professional oaths and therefore can NEVER be trusted in anything they say. But the Democrats will make a show out of it. We already know the result. They will find the president unstable emotionally with this or that psychiatric problem. Democrats will make a big deal out of this hit job against the president and use it as a reason for impeachment.

Remember, this action is completely consistent with Saul Alinsky's "Rules for Radicals", where he says in rule #13, Pick the target, (President Trump), freeze it, (meaning he is accused of having psychiatric problems with zero objective empirical evidence), then polarize it, meaning create accusations that he is crazy out of thin air. It DOES NOT MATTER if the accusations are true or not. Just make the accusations with psychiatrists of questionable character that will say what you want them to say. Disgusting but this is what Democrats are doing. Another lying hoax to create fear within the American population based on nothing of any validity. [81]

Summary: Inventing hoaxes and hiding reality by using soft words is an extremely vile and evil thing to do. It is Satanic to this writer for this sin destroys ever so many connections between people. It generates dis-trust between people, exactly the opposite of God's will for us. To the cruel and ignorant this produces occasions to create physical violence and physical harm to God's children. This is pure evil just as Satan likes it.

---

[81]   https://www.thedailysheeple.com/psychiatrists-willing-to-breach-professional-ethics-to-participate-in-house-democrats-event-scrutinize-trumps-mental-health/

4. **Democrats actively work against the health and wellbeing of American citizens**

   a. Alexandria Ocasio-Cortez Gives Illegal Aliens Tips on How to Evade ICE Raids. This is actually a felony crime to aid and assist criminal illegal aliens avoid

   b. Elizabeth Warren In Favor of 'Decriminalizing' Illegal Border Crossing. This means that anyone on our planet can now come to the US and claim government benefit paid for by the American taxpayer.

   c. Attacks citizen's wealth they earned. As Democrats Push "Wealth Tax," Here's Why Other Countries Got Rid of It [82]

   d. "Illegal immigrants should get health care, say Dems in Night 2 debate". In other words, Democrats want to take a lot more of your productive life's earnings and give it to people who do not belong here. [83]

   e. Medicare for all! Yippee! That would cost $93 Trillion or more in 10 years. This would bankrupt our country. This is a trojan horse that sounds nice to power hungry radicals and ignorant people but is a nation killer in costs to people. Democrats know this, they are perverted and Satanic driven but are not stupid. The evil is that they want to do this anyway to all of us.

   f. All Democrat presidential candidates are for giving the vote to all felons. They are also for radically reduced sentences for committing serious crimes and retain the rights to vote in elections. Does anyone in their right mind want criminals running our country? Democrats do because they know they are criminals and need other criminal support to gain political power.

   g. Democrat from New Mexico, Deb Haaland said that assault using hammers, bike locks and clubs against other people at a protest by Antifa is "peaceful". [84] So, if you or I did a job on Deb's head with her

---

[82]   https://www.zerohedge.com/news/2019-06-26/democrats-push-wealth-tax-heres-why-other-countries-got-rid-it

[83]   https://www.foxnews.com/politics/democrat-presidential-candidates-favor-health-care-coverage-for-undocumented-immigrants

[84] Fox News, Tucker Carlson, August 19, 2019,

"peaceful hammer", I guess she would not complain. 472 people were murdered by blunt objects in 2016.

Summary: The first and foremost duty of any government is to protect its people from outside harm, to protect their health and wellbeing. This is number one. Every action taken in congress by Democrats has been aimed at doing exactly the opposite and directly against the American citizens.

Democrats have purposely and willfully supported a policy of allowing the entire world to come here and get free housing, free food, free clothing and free medical care. This is ALL PAID FOR BY THE OVERTAXED AMERICAN CITIZEN. This destroys and illegally confiscates more and more of the productive sacred live of everyone of God's children, and substantially increases deadly crime against citizens but also brings huge quantities of drugs into our country and since most of these illegal aliens are not vaccinated, bring more disease with them as well. Los Angeles now has a typhoid epidemic on their hands.

h. **Headline: Kamala Harris: 'I am a gun owner' for personal protection.**

Boy! We are demonized by the stinking Democrat party but they can have guns for personal protection but we taxpayers cannot. HYPOCRICY! [85]

5. **Attack Our Country Directly, Democrat Party and ANTIFA**

   a. Cory Booker: *American Capitalism Is 'Perverted'* [86]

   b. *"Our founding fathers were not living gods...they were fallible human beings." The Declaration of Independence "did not condemn slavery, protect the rights of women or include Native Americans."* Ayanna Pressley.[87]

   c. *"American was never that great"*, Gov. Cuomo N.Y.

[85] The Hill, BY RACHEL FRAZIN - 04/11/19 04:03 PM EDT

[86] https://www.breitbart.com/clips/2019/06/26/cory-booker-american-capitalism-is-perverted/

[87] https://thefederalistpapers.org/opinion/leftists-celebrate-independence-day-burning-declaration-independence-american-flag

d. *Leftists Celebrate Independence Day by Burning Declaration of Independence, American Flag.* [88]

e. *Fourth of July's ugly truth exposed: The Declaration of Independence is sexist, racist, prejudiced.* [89] Really? How? This leftist rant is complete BS. When asked, a Democrat can never answer the above question of "How?". In this case, how is our beloved Declaration of Independence sexist, or racist or prejudiced? They cannot answer this question because our founding documents are God inspired aimed at freeing ALL peoples from tyranny.

f. *Here's what Douglass has to say about the Founders: "Fellow Citizens, I am not wanting in respect for the fathers of this republic. The signers of the Declaration of Independence were brave men. They were great men too — great enough to give fame to a great age. It does not often happen to a nation to raise, at one time, such a number of truly great men. The point from which I am compelled to view them is not, certainly, the most favorable; and yet I cannot contemplate their great deeds with less than admiration. They were statesmen, patriots and heroes, and for the good they did, and the principles they contended for, I will unite with you to honor their memory. ..."*

[88] https://thefederalistpapers.org/opinion/leftists-celebrate-independence-day-burning-declaration-independence-american-flag

[89] https://www.salon.com/2019/07/04/fourth-of-julys-ugly-truth-exposed-the-declaration-of-independence-is-sexist-racist-and-prejudice/

*"They were peace men; but they preferred revolution to peaceful submission to bondage. They were quiet men; but they did not shrink from agitating against oppression. They showed forbearance; but that they knew its limits. They believed in order; but not in the order of tyranny. With them, nothing was "settled" that was not right. With them, justice, liberty and humanity were "final;" not slavery and oppression. You may well cherish the memory of such men. They were great in their day and generation. **Their solid manhood stands out the more as we contrast it with these degenerate times.** " Fredrick Douglass* [90]

g. So, Rashida Tlaib was just contradicted by none other than Alexandria Ocasio-Cortez, courtesy of the great Frederick Douglass.

h. **CNN's Chris Cuomo Defends Left-wing Terrorist Group Antifa as *'Good Cause'*** [91] Imagine voting for this leftist band of punks that have an avalanche of hate in their hearts against all that is good in our

country. Does anyone really want to vote for the Democrats who support this Satanic mob of haters. The above is what Chris Cuomo thinks is a good cause. Why do they hide their faces? This is just what Satan did when he tempted Adam and Eve. He appeared as a snake. If a snake is an improvement in his looks, just imagine what he really must look like. Probably something like Hillary Clinton. Ouch! This is just what the KKK did too.

---

[90] https://www.thenation.com/article/what-slave-fourth-july-frederick-douglass/
[91] https://www.blabber.buzz/conservative-news/605674-nolte-cnns-chris-cuomo-defends-left-wing-terrorist-group-antifa-as-good-cause-special

Ever wonder where this radical leftist hate group and others like it get funded? Why are these people not working at a job instead of rioting and protesting all the time? The answer is one of Satan's main minions…George Soros. More on this future resident of hell later on.

i. *Antifa Plots Acid Attack at DC Free Speech Rally* [92]. For exercising their rights of free speech, antifa wants to blind people for disagreeing with them. Now please think about just what kind of person does it take to want to throw acid in the face of another human being just because they have a different political viewpoint. Also think about the fact that at least to my extensive knowledge, NOT ONE DEMOCRAT HAS CONDEMMED ANTIFA for anything they have done regarding all the damage they have caused. Not one!

j. *KERNS: Antifa Has Shown Why It Should Be Designated A Domestic Terror Group* [93] Antifa feeds on fear. They want to be feared and want to attack anything that represents "We the People" in the United States and dominate God's children through mob action and force against people who want "life, liberty and pursue happiness".

k. **"Nazi Scum!" at Senior Woman with a Walker Outside Dave Rubin Event in Canada** [94] Far left antifa thugs harassed, blocked and screamed "Nazi scum!" at a senior woman with a walker outside of Dave

Rubin's event with Maxime Bernier in Hamilton, Ontario. Democrats to my knowledge have never called out ANTIFA for their brutality to ever so many of God's children.

---

[92] https://www.zerohedge.com/news/2019-07-01/antifa-plots-acid-attack-dc-free-speech-rally

[93] https://dailycaller.com/2019/07/01/kerns-antifa-terror/

[94] https://www.blabber.buzz/conservative-news/667548-antifa-thugs-harass-block-and-scream-nazi-scum-at-senior-woman-with-a-walker-outside-dave-rubin-event-in-canada-video?utm_source=c-mid&utm_medium=c-mid-email&utm_term=c-mid-GI

1. ICE releases list of accused murderers, rapists protected under state's sanctuary law. These are illegal aliens that attacked and killed American citizens. Democrats all across our nation actively work against the children of God in this country to protect illegal alien criminals from our justice system. I never thought I would see this day come to our country. Every child of God must realize who we are really fighting. It is Satan working through evil minded humans which is a situation as old as the hills.

   Summary: The Democrat party has been forced into showing its true colors, it's true morality and foundational principles. The Democrat party is one of Satanic negativity with an obsessive loss for political power and dominion over God's children living in the United States. It is painful for me to have to reveal this conclusion and truth for one of our two major political parties. I promised God I would follow the truth wherever it takes me. The truth of the matter is that the Democrats have given themselves over to the forces of evil and the dark side of human nature.

   And, it is always for the same reason. It is the reason that Satan rebelled against Almighty God's heavenly kingdom. Satan wanted dominion over God's kingdom. That word "dominion" can be a terrible word. It means the opposite of servitude. It is servitude that God wants all of his children to be in light of all his other children. We are to serve the needs of our brothers and sisters.

   We are expressly forbidden from seeking dominion over others in our sacred brotherhood. Yet this is precisely what Satan wanted and it is precisely what the Democrat party wants, again it is dominion and control over God's children, not servitude. The servitude comes from our heartfelt love for God's other children which we do freely from our hearts.

6. **They attack people that they disagree with**

   a. *Antifa Plans Acid Attack on D.C. Free Speech Rally, Promises to Blind Attendees* [95]

---

[95] https://www.thedailysheeple.com/antifa-plans-acid-attack-on-d-c-free-speech-rally-promises-to-blind-attendees/

b. Constant accusations against President Trump. He is a racist, homophobe, xenophobe, bigot, misogynist, hateful, white supremacist and abuser along with every other insult that can be thought of. This is consistent with Saul' Alinsky's book, Rules for Radicals where he advises to always keep the pressure on no matter what.

c. *"AOC: Trump Supporters Aren't Educated Enough to Realize They're Racist"*, Source: TheNewAmerican | August 17, 2019 11:06 AM [96]

d. Everybody they don't like is automatically a racist. *"Ocasio Cortez Furious, Team Accuses Pelosi, Dems Of Being Racists."* [97] Democrat calls other Democrats a racist. Nobody is safe.

e. Todd Starnes: Portland's mayor has turned his city over to Antifa thugs, assault journalist [98] They are out of control.

f. 'Squad' Member Rep. Ayanna Pressley (D-Mass.) Calls Mitch McConnell 'Common Enemy' Amid Left-Wing Death Threats. just a week after far-left activists surrounded the Senate Majority Leader's house threatening to "stab the motherfucker in the heart. [99]

g. 'Mini AOC' ends parody videos after receiving 'death threats,' 'harassment' from the left, family says. The 8-year-old child actor who went viral for impersonating Rep. Alexandria Ocasio-Cortez, D-NY,

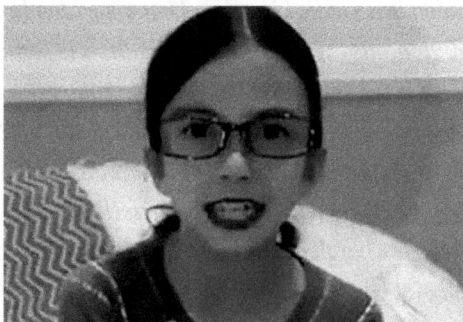

is no longer going to make videos due to death threats and harassment she and her family have

---

[96] https://www.blabber.buzz/conservative-news/638885-aoc-trump-supporters-arent-educated-enough-to-realize-theyre-racist-special?utm_source=c-mid&utm_medium=c-mid-email&utm_term=c-mid-Yahoo

[97] https://www.blabber.buzz/conservative-news/605285-ocasio-cortez-furious-team-accuses-pelosi-dems-of-being-racists-special?utm_source=c-am&utm_medium=c-am-email&utm_term=c-am-Yahoo

[98] https://www.foxnews.com/opinion/todd-starnes-antifa-portland-mayor

[99] https://www.blabber.buzz/conservative-news/636308-squad-member-calls-mitch-mcconnell-common-enemy-amid-left-wing-death-threats-special?utm_source=c-pm&utm_medium=c-pm-email&utm_term=c-pm-Yahoo

received. [100] Look at the picture of "mini AOC" and realize that leftist have threatened to kill this beautiful little girl for being on TV and imitating AOC. They want to kill her, a child of God. Do you want to vote for any politician that is associated with death threats against a 12 year old girl just because she imitates a democrat nominee?

Summary: bankrupt ideologies like socialism, like communism, like dictatorships and like tyranny all must be forced upon the common people. These political ideologies can only survive if there are a lot of guns in the hands of the government, no guns in the hands of the people.

Remember, the second amendment is not for hunting turkeys. It is to provide self-protection to every citizen of our country from both crime and the government. Our founding fathers knew that government naturally becomes corrupt over time. It is only sufficient weaponry in the hands of the citizenry that is our ultimate protection against government tyranny which always seems to surface as time goes on in any country including the United States.

We right now as a country have a colossal corruption problem in all levels of our government. The level of corruption is astounding beyond belief. But it is there as we have seen in recent events like the Russian collusion hoax by the Democrats. Like the latest Clinton body count which has risen to 80 people now who have been killed by mysterious means all of whom had intimate knowledge of the corruption controlled by Bill and Hillary Clinton. We now have a Department of Justice that just might be honest enough to clean its own house and drove those guilty parties in jail of which I believe there are many.

In a backhanded way it is good that the Democrats tried their Russian collusion hoax and failed. This was a political coup attempt which is complete treason in our country. But now because of its failure we have the names of the people who played an active role in trying to take down our American government for the purpose of continuing horrific corruption at the highest levels of our federal government.

Make no mistake however, Satanic corruption against God's children is ever present at all levels of government including state and local as well as police forces, the FBI, the DOJ, the DHS, the IRS and other government agencies. Government at all levels in our country have reached the point where every one of them needs a

---

[100] https://www.foxnews.com/entertainment/mini-aoc-ends-parody-videos-after-receiving-death-threats-harassment-from-left

gigantic enema to clean out all the corruption and dishonesty that prevails in our government today.

Beware, there will be much violence in the coming months before the 2020 presidential election. I predict that Donald Trump will be reelected and that will serve as a trigger for even more bloody violence in our beloved country the United States.

7. **Democrats like death from abortion but call it something else.**

I honestly cannot fathom and understand how any human being can willfully and purposely kill an unborn child. This is an abomination against Almighty God, creator of all that is seen and unseen. This subject is central to God's plan for all of His children on this earth.

Yet Democrats are all for abortion at any time any place for any reason. Killing and death of the unborn babies just does not bother these heartless assassins of children. Death just does not mean much to Democrats as they confirm this assessment every time they open their Satanic mouths. I personally condemn them for this policy and attitude they have.

They have this in common with Muslims. Many times, I have seen and read articles about how much "Muslims crave death".

Headline: *L.A. Students Enthusiastically Sign Petition To Protect Unborn Eagles; But When It Comes To Unborn Babies, Well…Watch* [101] [102]

---

[101]   https://www.redstate.com/elizabeth-vaughn/2019/09/05/l.a.-students-enthusiastically-sign-petition-protect-unborn-eagles-comes-unborn-babies-well...watch
[102] https://youtu.be/ZR9Ye_Uk-x8

Prager University's Will Witt asks students in the Echo Park neighborhood of Los Angeles to sign a petition supporting the protection of unborn eagles. All are happy to sign. Then, he tells them about his "other" petition which supports the rights of unborn babies. They quickly lose their enthusiasm. The students quickly reverted to the Democrat abortion mantra of "women's reproductive health" and "women's right to choose".

These leaders of tomorrow place more importance and rights to survival on an unborn bird that they do "developing fetal human beings", unborn babies in other words. What a twisted evil set of values that have been propagandized into their brains. Remember that Satan is the prince of this world and does indeed have influence over people.

Abortion AFTER Birth:

It is being proposed on the east coast that it is now legal to murder a baby already born. After birth the mother, doctor and whomever decide whether or not to kill the newborn baby. This is pure Satanic thought under the guise of something else. Remember, this falls under the category of "women's reproductive health". If there is one thing Satan loves, it is the murder of a developing fetal human being in the womb or better yet, kill the baby AFTER it is born. Yeah Democrats. Of course, they cloak (hide) their true intentions of wanting to destroy the children of God as Satan demands by lying and calling it "women's reproductive rights".

Because of Democrats in our country, since the court case of Roe vs. Wade, there have been 50 million killings of unborn "developing fetal human beings" in a mother's womb. Just think of the horror of this. Does this statistic shock you. I hope so because that means you value the priceless life that God gives to us here on earth. You are reading this paragraph only because YOUR MOTHER DID NOT HAVE YOU ABORTED! Remember this.

Do not fall for the related lie regarding the false controversy about "when does life begin". All that is "BULLSHOOT". From a pure biological and scientific perspective, life begins when the egg is fertilized by the sperm. This is medical fact and not an opinion. If anyone says different, either they are ignorant or have an evil agenda. There really is nothing in between.

Time to think for a moment. Real medical emergencies aside, how in the hell does killing a fetus or newborn baby increase the "reproductive health" of the mother? IT DOES NOT! This is a Satanic lie of monster proportion. Doctors anywhere will tell you that the claim of "women's reproductive health" has nothing to do with killing an innocent developing fetal human being…NOTHING! This is all a big LIE from the mouths of Democrats. Said in crude terms, "you can call a turd a meadow muffin if you want, but it still remains a turd".

Summary:

A fetus in the womb is most accurately described as a "developing fetal human being". It is an unborn human being right after fertilization of the egg. This state of existence for humans is a direct creation of Almighty God. Unlike others in God's creation like angels, humans can procreate. Angels cannot. Human's can co-create with God. This is fantastic but something we do not think of in this way as we should. Satan wants to destroy all of God's human children, all of us.

Killing babies in the womb using the LIE of "women's reproductive health or rights", is the way of pure evil. Therefore, it is easy to see that the Democrat party is doing the work of Satan.

8. **Democrats have an awful time with gender:**

   They fail to be able to count up to two genders. They do not know how many genders there is and are not starting to teach this rot to our children in school. This creates tension between the sexes. God said they will be male and female. Simple.

   a. Tensions between trans women and gay men boil over at Stonewall anniversary. This is a headline where sexually mixed up people argued over God knows what. My question is were the trans women actually men wanting to be women or women wanting to be a man. What a mess.

   b. Want kids to chose which sex they are. Are these people nuts? Yes! At that age I just wanted to avoid school and play with my friends.

   c. *"It's important to remember that gender identity is not visible -- it's an internal sense of one's own gender," the left-wing Human Rights*

Campaign (HRC) claims.[103] Gone are the days when a child only need to look into their pants to find out what their gender is. Nope, much more complex than that now thanks to Democrats. This crappy ideology goes along with trying to purge "maleness" out of young boys and make them into "psycho-girls". Please see this for what it is, a plain frontal attack against the very structure of human existence as determined by Almighty God. Simply put, this is a Satanic attempt to destroy the fact that God's human children are made in His image. Now Democrats want to work with Satan to destroy the image of God's children and change it into a Satan inspired image instead. This is the mark of pure evil.

d.   This is a Satanic attempt to destroy one of the foundational elements that God has set forth for His Children, to come together in love from which new life can spring forth in the image of God and the two parents. We are co-creators of humankind with Almighty God.

Summary: Ever since creation, mankind is made of men and women. It is part of the very foundation of human existence. Satan wants to attack the very structure of our existence and make it into some perverted mess inspired by him. Look at all the messed up people running around now not sure of their own gender which is a man made chaotic pile of confusing pronouns and special rules for this, that and the other thing. This is part of "confusing the enemy" as described by Saul Alinsky in his book, "Rules for Radicals".

9.   Democrats do NOT like free speech at all! They Want to Control What You Say:

a.   Frederica Wilson: We Must Prosecute Anyone Who 'Makes Fun' Of Members of Congress Online[104]

b.   *"The Democrats' bill violates the First Amendment. It restricts political speech and election activities in several ways that the U.S. Supreme Court has made crystal clear violates the Constitution, such as groups' pooling resources to take out ads on the issues those groups advocate".*

---

[103] https://www.lifesitenews.com/news/four-cis-2020-democrats-add-preferred-gender-pronouns-to-campaign-twitter-bios

[104] Frederica Wilson: We Must Prosecute Anyone Who 'Makes Fun' Of Members Of Congress Online

c.   Headline: *"Pelosi Votes to Take Away Constitutional Right – Sabotage a Win in 2020." Pelosi's legislation is a massive federal power grab away from the states. The Constitution gives primary authority to the sovereign states to conduct elections. This bill empowers the federal government to micromanage elections.* [105] This would give way too much power to a central figure. This is completely against the constitution and frankly the will of God as He created us as individuals and sovereign.

d.   Headline: *"Every Democrat in the Senate Supports a Constitutional Amendment That Would Radically Curtail Freedom of Speech* [106]

e.   *The Democracy for All Amendment aims to mute some voices so that others can be heard."* [107]

f.   Headline: *San Francisco Wants to Change What Criminals are Called. Source San Francisco Chronicle.* [108]Remember this dear reader, if you wish to control people's thoughts you must first control their vocabulary. This is EXACTLY what the Democrats are pushing for in our entire country. If you do not have the words to express yourself, then you have become neutered and ideas cannot be dealt with. Good ideas will never be able to spread and implemented. Democrats want to control your mind and your tongue. This is pure Satanic evil. God has given each of us free will which mean a free mind and free expression. The Democrats are working hard to combat the will of Almighty God who is the creator of all things seen and unseen. This can ONLY BE COMING FROM SATAN through the evil ones that walk with us on this earth.

San Francisco with all its dirty filth of disease spreading through the streets now like a plague of rats spreading typhus, measles etc. wants to hide the objective truth of things by eliminating common words that accurately describe things. Here are some horrific examples.

---

[105]   https://capitalhill.org/2019/01/30/pelosi-votes-to-take-away-constitutional-right-sabotage-a-win-in-2020/

[106]   https://reason.com/2019/08/12/every-democrat-in-the-senate-supports-a-constitutional-amendment-that-would-radically-curtail-freedom-of-speech/

[107]   https://reason.com/2019/08/12/every-democrat-in-the-senate-supports-a-constitutional-amendment-that-would-radically-curtail-freedom-of-speech/

[108]   http://forliberty.news/2019/08/22/san-francisco-wants-change-criminals-called/

a. A "convicted felon" is now called a "formerly incarcerated person" or a "justice involved" person or a "returning resident".

b. A parolee is now a "person under supervision".

c. A juvenile delinquent is now a "young person with justice involvement"

d. A drug addict is now a "person with a history of substance use".

Please notice that we will no longer be able to correctly understand people with criminal records as this mush mouth vocabulary is designed to cover over the truth of things as they really are. This is an evil gambit to hide truth. This goes directly against God and Jesus Christ who is "the way, the truth and the life". God is truth and Democrats are working exactly against this. Only Satan can be the root cause of this kind of monstrosity. I have dealt with Satan and some of his demons in my life. I know what I am speaking of.

Summary: *God has given all of us his children a free will. This is an undeniable blessing for bringing his brotherhood of children together in a free exchange of ideas and thoughts. Any attempt by anybody like Satan or Democrats restrict the free expression of ideas in public works against God's will for his children and stifles both the physical and spiritual growth of his children and the reason we came to earth in the first place. Democrats in their satanic lust for dominion want to also control our thoughts and the expression of our thoughts. Deep inside Democrats know they are headed for extinction through the normal political process and the ever increasing understanding of human beings with God. This lust for dominion drives them toward attempting to control every aspect of human life while we are on this planet. It is only through dominion, control of speech and thoughts, and other force fit structures aimed to restrict and dominate every aspect of our lives can the Democrats achieve the political power they so cravenly lust for.*

If liberty means anything at all, it means the right to tell people what they do not want to hear. George Orwell

10. **Gun Control:** Democrats constantly attack our inalienable God given right to protect ourselves from harm. They repeatedly attack the 2nd amendment to destroy our legal rights to bear firearms.

We must all remember that everyone has a "God given right to life which means the ability for self-defense". In our modern world this means firearms. This right is NOT given by government. It is from Almighty God Himself. This right is even recognized by John Locke, English philosopher considered to be the "Father of Liberalism".

"I should have a right to destroy that which threatens me with destruction: for, by the fundamental law of nature, man being to be preserved as much as possible, when all cannot be preserved, the safety of the innocent is to be preferred." John Locke, August 1632 – 28 October 1704)

Remember the reason for this amendment is twofold. First to protect ourselves from harm from criminals. The second reason is to protect ourselves from our government. You need firepower for that. Also remember that it is the American citizen that retains ultimate sovereignty over our country, NOT our government. The Democrat vision is that nobody has any kid of gun, only government police do. Every time in human history when the people do not have guns, this is followed by complete government tyranny and mass genocide. China, Russia, Laos, Viet Nam, Cuba, Germany and so on.

a. "Kamala Calls for 'Domestic Terrorism Prevention Orders' to Seize Guns from White Nationalists." [109] Question: What is her definition of a White Nationalist? How do you know if a person is or not? What does a person need to say or due to have that label? Disgusting.

b. Chuck Schumer Wants to Restrict Access to Body Armor: 'Wares of War Demand FBI Checks'. Apparently Chucky wants more people to die from gunshot wounds.

c. *"The Second Amendment only protects the people who want all the guns they can have. The rest of us, we've got no Second Amendment. What are we supposed to do?"* Rep. Louise Slaughter (D-New York) in a March 12 interview with John Fugelsang on Current TV's "Viewpoint." This is completely nonsensical. Can anyone understand what she said?

d. *"Well, you know, my shotgun will do better for you than your AR-15, because you want to keep someone away from your house, just fire the*

---

109 https://www.gunsamerica.com/digest/kamala-calls-for-domestic-terrorism-prevention-orders-to-seize-guns-from-white-nationalists/?utm_source=email&utm_medium=20190816_FridayDigest_239&utm_campaign=/digest/kamala-calls-for-domestic-terrorism-prevention-orders-to-seize-guns-from-white-nationalists/

shotgun through the door." The FAMOUS JOE BIDEN STUPID QUOTE OF TIME.

e. *"If I could have banned them all -- 'Mr. and Mrs. America turn in your guns' -- I would have!"* Famous Diane Feinstein quote. [110]

f.

11. **Democrats are "anti-white", anti-Jewish and "anti-male" these days.** Somehow the Democrat Party has calculated that the best way to get elected in 2020 is to attack "white people". Now remember Democrats call people "racists" all the time, the ones they disagree with. Now they are being openly racist against white people. But you will never hear Democrats say they are the racists they really are.

Democrats have been busy trying to distort, mutate and revise the truth of our beloved country's history. Whether or not Democrats like this, the objective facts are that the people who created the United States of America are European white people of all different kinds. WHITE PEOPLE CREATED AND BUILT THIS GREAT NATION THE UNITED STATES OF AMERICA. Millions came here from all different places in Europe to create a land of freedom. They suffered, they worked endlessly, they died in great numbers due to the very harsh conditions but continued onward in the face of great hardships over many years. It is because of European white people speaking different languages coming from different cultures that we have the best country ever known in the history of mankind. Instead of being thankful as they should be, Democrats want to tear down the achievements of our founding fathers and all the pioneers of our country into a heap of lies, distortions and hateful narratives.

Even as white racism has become a phenomenon of the insignificant fringe the left's accusations of white racism have escalated to the point of terminal absurdity. Thus, Black Lives Matter and other progressive voices describe America as a "white supremacist nation." This accusation is made against a country that outlaws racial discrimination, that has twice elected a black president, has recently had a black four-star general head of the Joint Chiefs of Staff, two black secretaries of state, three black national security advisors and two successive black attorneys

---

[110]   https://www.outdoorlife.com/blogs/gun-shots/2013/07/9-dumbest-gun-control-quotes-politicians-and-celebrities/

general along with thousands of black elected officials, mayors, police chiefs and congressmen. [111]

a. Democrat Rep. Shelia Jackson Lee from Texas made the case for reparations for the descendants of slaves in part because of President Trump's behavior. Now lets think about this. Somehow, she thinks that because of her emotions regarding what she calls President Trumps behavior now is the time to charge reparation money on white people. There is no connection between President Trump and slavery so long ago, but this does not deter her from demanding money from white people today. This absolutely makes no sense at all. But never mind that. She thinks that your white great great great great grandpa might have own slaves of the great great great black grandsons and granddaughters living today. Never mind that there is nobody living today that was either a slave or a slave owner. Never mind that slavery still exists in the world today and that hundreds of thousands of white people died to free slaves in this country. She wants black people today to be paid money for being black. She wants white people today to pay the black people. Why? It is because they may be the decedents of slaves hundreds of years ago. White people in her twisted mind are responsible today for what might have happened hundreds of years ago. Now in my case, my ancestors arrived in America in 1905. There was no slaver then. Am I supposed to pay just because I am white? This woman is a complete racist and bigot. But because she is Democrat, she will never be called that.

b. Dem Rep. Wilson: *"Detention Centers Led by 'White Men' Who Use Facilities as 'Money Making Scheme".* The picture they are promoting is complete racial division between white people and other people. This is right out of Satan's playbook, to seed division and hatred among the people. It is also right out of "Rules for Radicals" by Godless communist rebel Saul Alinsky where he promotes the idea that the end does indeed justify the means no matter how dishonest or cruel or how

[111] https://www.breitbart.com/the-media/2016/04/26/anti-white-racism-hate-dares-not-speak-name-2/

many people it injures the means are. [112] This "ends justify the means" is on pages 24-47.

I ask the very serious question, "does anyone in their right mind want to have people in our government that are openly racist against white people and males and use a radical communist playbook to define their ethics and political tactics?" If you do, there are a whole host of countries in South America and Africa that you will like very much. Go there! I will pay for your one-way ticket.

c. *"You f*cking Jew b@stard."* – Hillary Clinton to political operative Paul Fray. This was revealed in "State of a Union: Inside the Complex Marriage of Bill and Hillary Clinton" and has been verified by Paul Fray and three witnesses. [113] If you ever voted for Hillary, this is the Satanic evil you voted for. Think about it dear reader.

d. *"I want to go up to the closest white person and say: 'You can't understand this, it's a black thing' and then slap him, just for my mental health."* -- Charles Barron, a New York city Democrat councilman at a reparations rally, 2002. [114]

e. *"Civil rights laws were not passed to protect the rights of white men and do not apply to them."* – Democrat Mary Frances Berry, Chairwoman, US Commission on Civil Rights.

f. *"White folks was in caves while we was building empires... We taught philosophy and astrology and mathematics before Socrates and them Greek homos ever got around to it."* – Democrat Rev. Al Sharpton in a 1994 speech at Kean College, NJ. Good God, Al cannot even speak proper English much less show any kind of love toward his fellow mankind and he calls himself a reverend. Not to mention the fact that his history of black people is completely wrong in every way.

[112] Rules for Radicals, Saul Alinsky, pg24-36. Vintage Books, 1971
[113] https://www.liveleak.com/view?i=ebd_1378232577
[114] IBID

Democrat 2020 Platform: [115]

Based on the Democrat candidate's rhetoric this is the 2020 Platform. These following completely self-destructive ideas have been gathered just by listening to the 2020 Democrat presidential candidates. Never in my life have I seen such asinine, such anti-American, such hateful proposals from any adult human beings.

Everything in the list below has been promoted by at least several of the Democrat presidential candidates. Because of how ridiculous these proposals are you may be tempted to think that this is invented are made up. It is NOT! This is the real thing.

If anyone dares to vote Democrat in the 2020 election this is what they are going to get. These ideas go against everything the United States of America stands for. There can be only one source for the depth of the hatred these proposals will bring to the children of God that live in the United States of America. That source can be none other than Satan and his minions. Remember that all of us Christians are fighting against,

These are a few of the planks to be considered in their 2020 convention platform:
- scare the hell out of voters so they won't vote Republican
- allow new born children to be murdered and call it late term abortion
- be anti-God
- be anti-Christian
- be anti-constitutional
- eliminate the 1st and 2nd Amendments
- have a two-tiered justice system
- enforce the religion of Global Warming bogus science
- eliminate health insurance
- have government run medical system
- be anti-Israel
- be anti-Male
- be anti-White Male
- support radical Muslim religions
- favor illegal aliens over US Citizens
- deny border crisis and eliminate borders
- give illegal aliens Constitutional rights
- allow terrorists to vote

---

[115] https://www.conservativedailynews.com/2019/05/breaking-heres-the-democrats-new-2020-platform/

- allow rapist and murderers to vote
- allow illegal aliens to vote
- eliminate middle America votes
- eliminate combustion engines
- eliminate airplanes
- eliminate vehicles
- eliminate ships
- eliminate farming
- eliminate cows
- rebuild all current buildings
- destroy and/or eliminate law enforcement
- impeach President Trump
- raise taxes
- replace Capitalism with Socialism

If Hillary Clinton Was Elected President:

Hillary!? OMG NO!!!!

A Hillary Clinton presidency would be an outright disaster for country. This would be true for anyone that has more than two brains cells rubbing together. After four years and hopefully not eight years our country would never be the same as the policies of Barack Obama would be largely continued. Along with the horrific enrichment through treason, fraud and other means, the Clinton family would have a good shot at becoming billionaires by doing such things as selling 20% of our nation's uranium reserves to the Russians. Oh…Hillary already did that. It is treason but the dark forces in the swamp refuse to administer the law when it comes to Magic Hillary. She did say in an interview that if she was charged with a crime, she could take "half of Washington" with her. Well…GREAT! Lets do just that!

Please figure out how it could possibly be that on the one side Hillary Clinton made $145 million in a payment to the Clinton foundation as a result of the uranium sale when Hillary was Secretary of State. And then, in the next breath she joined the radical Democrat socialist choir in condemning Pres. Donald Trump during the Russian collusion hoax and calling Russia a terrible evil in the world. If you can reconcile those two thoughts, you are a leftist Democrat with no brains.

Since Hillary can be bought, there is no telling what policies she would really implement as money is being paid to her under the table. That being said if you take a look at her 2020 campaign and what she said, the following is what can be reasonably expected to have happened if it ever was president Hillary Clinton. These are only the big promises with wide impact.

1. All sorts of social perversions would come to the front of the news. Things like "cultural appropriation" which is a "heinous crime against humanity". It is when you use some facet of another culture in for example clothes you wear. I committed this terrible crime when I got married to a wonderful Philippine woman years ago. During the wedding ceremony, I wore the traditional Filipino shirt called a Barong. In doing so I was GUILTY of cultural appropriation according to our cultural police. Stupid isn't it.

2. There would be a vast increase in "investigations" of Republicans for everything under the sun. Just like the HOAX Mueller Russian Collusion investigation, you can count on many more investigations using government power to persecute political enemies.

3. All illegal aliens in this country today will have formalized government benefits and support. They would be well on their way to becoming citizens with everything that entails. The effect of this would be there would be an additional 10 million to 20 million Democrat voters in our country. Think about this. This will complete the lustful power grab of the Democrats in such a way that conservativism would be considered a terrorist activity.

4. Because of number one above having a monstrously large increase in the number of ignorant voters in our country who are indebted to the government for their livelihoods, there are a number of probable government policies that would be implemented.

    a. There would be a mandatory national registry of all owners of weapons of any kind.

    b. The AR 15 rifle is not an assault rifle nor military rifle. It however will become an endangered species very likely subjected to very heavy taxes.

    c. To own one, or any other gun, a draconian background check which would be expanded to invade the private lives of anyone who wants to own a weapon. Millions of dollars of propaganda money will be spent to demonize anyone that owns a gun.

    d. Our police forces will be weakened significantly more than they already are. They will continue to be demonized as black people haters and other such Satanic inspired phrases. We will see a further decrease in the number of police to protect American citizens.

e. Because of the legalization of all illegal aliens our southern border will constantly hemorrhage with millions more people coming here every year. They will all be entitled to full government benefits.

f. Current illegal aliens will gain the right to vote. Just think of an extra 10 million to 20 million more votes for Democrats. We will never again have a Judeo-Christian government. It will be a Satan-fest!

g. This is the kind of headline that we will see lots more of. *The Baltimore County Police Department announced recently that seven suspects, were charged with killing 21-year-old Daniel Alejandro Alvarado Cuellar. Six of the seven people charged in the stabbing death of a man in Maryland have been identified as being part of the MS-13 gang and in the country illegally. Police have reported that brutal killings by MS-13 Gang Members have been on the rise in 2019.* [116]

h. MS-13 has as many as 10,000 members in the United States and is active in at least 40 states. Vote Democrat if you like the looks of the above killers in your neighborhood. Remember what Nancy Pelosi said about people like the above, "they are God's children with a divine sparkle in their heart". BULLSHOOT!

i. Many new government programs will need to be implemented at tremendous cost to the American people. These new government

[116] https://www.foxnews.com/us/ms13-gang-members-illegal-immigrants-maryland-stabbing-deadly-ice

programs will include building new infrastructure for all the illegal alien citizens. The list of new spending will become enormous and it will necessitate an absolutely huge tax increase upon all of American God's children who have any income.

j. Currently 47% of the individuals that live in this country pay no federal income tax. With all the newly minted illegal aliens in the country, that percentage will increase to something well above 50%. This will cause tremendous resentment on the part of existing taxpayers as their taxes will increase dramatically. This is of no concern to Democrats because it is part of their mindset to not care about what happens to "the other guy".

k. Middle class taxes will go up in direct opposition to promises Hillary made during the campaign. It will be another President Bush read my lips moment.

l. Minimum wage laws will become far more comprehensive and the minimum wage will increase. This will certainly have two bad effects. Minimum wage jobs will decrease thus secondly it will result in increasing unemployment.

m. Many steps will be taken behind the scenes in the political world to further cement the Democrat hold on all levels of government. New rules will be put into place that will make it far harder to oppose the existing government and its policies. Our country will have become a tyrannical oligarchy.

n. The Constitution will be declared obsolete. Everything bad that this entails will happen or be in the process of happening.

o. We will probably be at war with North Korea. This is especially true if the Clintons can figure out how to make money on the deal. This will be a particularly deadly war and long-lasting. It is no joke to say that total casualties will range well into the millions. This is because of the huge size of the North Korean army. They may even get assistance from China because Hillary Clinton will also demonize China in addition to Russia. If North Korea has a hidden nuclear bomb purchased from Pakistan or India or even Russia, they will use it on the American "invaders". South Korea will probably be the recipient.

p. Our relationship with Russia will go down the toilet. Not because it's necessary for our security, but only because it's popular with the Democrat political base. The mindset of radical liberals requires that there always be a boogeyman somewhere. It would never occur to anyone in the Democrat administration to actually talk with North Korea and negotiate peace. It would never occur to a Democrat administration to offer to talk with Iran and our other enemies. Democrats are too damned stupid to know that talking piece avoids war and the probability of war. Why wouldn't they do this? The answer is ugly and simple. Politics and money. Democrats will make the political calculation that if we are at war people are more likely to vote for the incumbent Democrats. Secondly a huge number of under the table deals will have been implemented to where members of the Democrat leadership and party will get bribery payments from the war profits of our military industrial complex.

q. If you are a white male heterosexual, you will get tremendous social grief from the perverts in the Democrat party. Over a relatively small period of time, if you are white you will be discriminated against openly and without remorse. Why no remorse? It is simple and ugly. Democrats feel completely justified by their own twisted moral principles to do whatever their emotions tell them to no matter who or how many people it hurts or damages. My story about the gay guys and condoms in front of my house illustrates this completely.

r. We will see far more drag queens in various parades around the country.

s. Social unrest will increase dramatically. Social conditions will be such that white people will become targets of anybody who is not white because the Democrat said this is okay.

t. Our economy will be very weak just like it was during the eight years of the Obama circus. Obama's "new normal" will get more normal but at lower levels of economic activity along with more unemployment, and more government benefit checks arriving it mailboxes. But remember this is precisely the kind of society Democrats want. They want a huge central government with all pervasive power over the people.

u. You will be forced to depend upon the government for all your health care. They will make illegal any private health organizations. You will be required to adhere to every rule and regulation of which there will be a monstrous mountain of.

v. People with sex perversions will become the role models and heroes of our society. Gone will be the commandments of God regarding marriage.

w. Any images that invoke Almighty God might actually be made illegal. If not more and more statues, paintings and other Christian icons will disappear from public view. This is precisely what Satan wants very badly. The Democrats will give it to him.

The United States will experience a very negative world to live in. It will be featured by the following:

a. much higher inflation

b. much higher unemployment

c. unconstitutional laws will flourish

d. individual rights will be trampled especially if you are white and double so if you are a male

e. radical leftist policies will be implemented in an avalanche of turds

f. drug use will increase exponentially

g. far more cities will become urban hellholes

h. our military will be gutted and our national security put at serious risk

i. as a result of above hostile foreign powers will be far more actively shooting at Americans and our military

j. we will be at war with North Korea, Iran and other hostile nations such as Yemen.

k. There is a very good chance that there will be some type of conflict between the military of the United States in the military of Russia. Democrats must target Russia because of the Russian collusion hoax. They need to be able to say," see I told you Russia was bad".

l. Government intrusion and surveillance into our lives will go well beyond what George Orwell ever thought was possible. We will become much like China where they are implementing technology to track the behavior of every person, what they say and what they do. Based on your behavior you are given a credit score. People who behave like China's government wants them to get higher scores and more government benefits. If you score badly you can be effectively ousted from society because you will not be able to work or to buy anything. You will be banned from all contact in society. This is real and it is happening today in China. We will have that in the United States too. Think About This Real Hard.

m. The lowest form of life in the United States will become Christian white males.

n. Racism and conflicts between races will increase dramatically as so too will be the horrific violence every day of every week of every month of every year. Why? Because it is Satan's rules that have been implemented.

o. The lowest people on the totem pole of societal preference will be Christian white males. These are the very people whose ancestors suffered greatly over a long period of time in order to create a great country we live in today.

There'll be much suffering in many different ways by the people in the United States. Because of perverted and Satanic identity politics, just walking down the street will become far more dangerous your personal health and well-being. Your life will not be yours to a far greater degree than before because of socialist laws. If you are wealthy much will be taken from you. If you earn a lot of income, it does not matter that you already pay 70% of federal income taxes, you will be demonized as part of the problem and your taxes will increase even more.

In summary: Your sacred life will be taken from you and completely controlled by central government based on their priorities and not yours. You are simply a cog in a big wheel. If you are Christian, you are in deep doo doo. This is simply because Almighty God has set eternal rules in place that forbid almost everything the Democratic Party wants to do. You are out of your God given mind if you vote for one Democrat in 2020, no exceptions.

Almighty God has set eternal rules in place that forbid almost everything the Democratic Party wants to do. This is why they hate Christians

APPENDIX A

APPENDIX A Saul Alinsky

https://planetxnews.com/2015/07/31/all-of-saul-alinskys-8-levels-of-control-are-now-operating-in-america/

https://www.snopes.com/fact-check/communist-rules-for-revolution/

The following eight rules for creating a socialist/communist state has been attributed to Saul Alinsky and or the communists during the first world war. This list is NOT in Alinsky's book Rules for Radicals. The story about Allied troops discovering this list in Germany in 1919 is unsubstantiated. Besides, a number of these rules do not reflect the issues of the times during the early 1900's. Therefore, the original author and proper attribution is not available. But this list had to be generated by communists at some time well after WWI.

Nonetheless, the following eight rules has been in use around the world for a very long time by socialists and communists who want to take over the control of a legitimate government. It is always associated with radicals, socialists and communists desire to overthrow existing governments and turn countries into socialist/communist states with a huge central overpowering government where the citizens have no real God given human rights. Citizens become viewed only as productive wards of the state with no individual rights.

There are eight levels of control that must be obtained before you are able to create a social state.

1) Healthcare – Control healthcare and you control the people.

This is enormous power over every individual person. Medical care is central to human existence. You can set the rules for who gets and doesn't get proper medical care. Now Democrats want to get rid of private medical insurance and make everyone dependent on the policies of the federal government. Does anyone want their medical care controlled by a monstrous federal government bureaucracy? If you do, you are nuts.

2) Poverty – Increase the poverty level as high as possible; poor people are easier to control and will not fight back if you are providing everything for them to live. Poverty got worse during the Obama years. He made no real attempt to get people off government assistance. Why? Because making people dependent on the government makes them want to vote for the politicians that promise more free benefits aka. Democrats.

3) Debt – Increase the debt to an unsustainable level. That way you are able to increase taxes, and this will produce more poverty. Barack Husain Obama, aka. Barry Soweto doubled the national debt during his eight years in office. There were 43 presidents before him in the history of our country in the past 230 years. He purposely and willfully increased our national debt that totaled ALL the previous presidents before him. Increasing taxes makes all people poorer and in more need of assistance. This was his Satanic goal. Make people more dependent on government handouts. Give them back what you tax away and people will think you are being nice to them. The truth is just the opposite. It is a mechanism toward slavery as perpetrated by the Democrat party.

4) Gun control – Remove people's ability to defend themselves from the government. That way you are able to create a police state. At some point, people will catch on to these tactics and will rebel, but they will not be able to defend themselves from the hostile government forces. Unfortunately, in this world it is the people with the most and largest guns that control society.

5) Welfare – Take control of every aspect of people's lives (food, housing and income). After you have gutted people's ability to be self-sufficient and get them on welfare, you do indeed have total control over their lives.

6) Education – Take control of what people read and listen to; take control of what children learn in school. This has been happening in our country for the past 30 years. Kids are being indoctrinated into believing socialist propaganda under the guise of education. Our own country's history is being revised or ignored in favor of a liberal socialist agenda. This is especially true at the college level.

7) Religion – Remove the belief in God from the government and schools. Liberals, socialists and communists MUST remove God from our lives. The reason is that Christianity does indeed give all people an accurate foundational world view of mankind's place in this universe and articulates the spiritual morality that must be used in the affairs of all mankind. The Christian values fly directly against and in the face of liberal control over people. This means liberals must attack the presence of God in all public affairs and individual lives so as to secure control over all people. This is EXACTLY WHAT SATAN WANTS ever since he rebelled against Almighty God and now wants to destroy all of God's children on earth. Democrats today do just this. They

attack anyone who believes in God and they vote against Christian who has been nominated for high public service. This is what they have done to Brett Kavanaugh for the supreme court and a large list of other Christian nominees for hundreds of important positions of service to our country.

8) Class warfare – Divide the people into the wealthy and the poor. This will cause more discontent and it will be easier to take from (tax) the wealthy with the support of the poor. Democrats constantly complain that all of societies imbalances are because of that evil rotten top 1% of wage earners. Never mind that the truth is the top 10% of wage earners pay 70% of the income taxes. Also never mind that a full 47% of American citizens pay ZERO income tax. The idea here is to divide and conquer as is taught to all military people. This is indeed a warfare tactic perpetrated against the American people. Do you smell Satan in this? You should.

9) Promote the idea that all morality is relative. This is pure Satan at work. The universe has been created with absolute laws and rules of human conduct. Democrats continuously promote the idea that "express yourself for what is right for you is what is important". BS. New York mayor Bill De Blasio has said this very thing. "Come to New York and do your thing whatever that may be". We will have your back. Each person has their own "truth" so live that he says. Do whatever you want. In other words, there is no real morality.

Does any of this sound like what is happening to the United States?

This list merely simplified, clarified and detailed Vladimir Lenin's original scheme for world conquest by communism, under Russian rule.

Have you noticed that in all the above radical leftist policies there is absolutely no mention whatsoever about government serving the best interest of the people and what is good for them? Have you noticed that all of the above is nothing more than a scheme, a strategy of monster evil manipulation of all the children of God to create a political class that has absolute power over the people in such a manner that they become powerless against the hostile government that controls every aspect of their lives. All of this in the end amounts to a human existence of slavery to a monster central government with no individual freedoms.

Remember that God has bequeathed to all of us individual freedoms and responsibilities. Freedom cannot exist without responsibility. Democrats say there is no real responsibility. Hell is full of people who took no responsibility for their lives. Also remember it is Satan that hates God, hates God's children and constantly works against the plan of God for us His children. Satan wants to enslave all of us into a meaningless live of misery with no hope of escape. Right now in the history of mankind, it is Democrats that are the tool that Satan is using to accomplish his evil horrific goals against us.

A vote for a Democrat is a vote for Satan!

APPENDIX B

An Example of Racist Hate Spread by CNN
State of Hate
The Explosion of White Supremacy
Fareed Zakaria Special CNN July 4, 2019

In the last number of years I have observed the Democrat party shifted symphysis from middle-class working people and representing their health and well-being in the marketplace toward socialist leftist race based and gender-based issues and ideologies. In the process the Democrat party has reinvented something called identity politics. This basically means that you are to be treated according to the color of your skin and what your heritage may be.

This is a complete abomination against the will of God and is to be rejected completely by any thinking and living human being. Barack Obama was a master of identity politics and his specialty was pitting one group of people against another. This is Satanic in its ultimate origin as it puts one child of God against another in an effort to crack the human brotherhood that is created by God into pieces. This is one of Satan's goals after he was thrown out of the heavenly kingdom. Barack Obama in my opinion is one of Satan's handmaidens.

The latest in a long series of hate propaganda from the Democrats is a special report from CNN title state of hate. The pretense for this report stated right in the subtitle. CNN wants to promote the idea or the narrative that white people in this country constitute a rabid danger to people of color including Jewish people. They want to show that white people are to be feared and it is okay to hate them because CNN says they hate you.

Fareed Zakaria is the tool CNN has used in this instance to spread their hate propaganda in the form of a so-called special report on how white people are increasing their explosion of hate against minorities can Jewish people. The idea is very simple. CNN wants to promote fear and distrust between different American citizens. Their message is you better watch out or the white people will get you.

Let's look into the specifics of this so-called special on white supremacy and see what the details are.

"America is at war with itself". "An army of hate whose numbers are soaring and it's spreading across the world." "Fed by politicians." Then they show Pres. Trump speaking. Guilt by video association they are saying Trump is a racist without verbalizing that. The message is clear. Trump is white and if you are not white, he hates you.

"The fabric of the country calls for action". (Against the whites).

In 1960, 89% of the population was white. Of course, whites built this country into the greatest country on earth. Because of the immigration act of 1965 many people from foreign lands immigrated here and became citizens. It is estimated that in 2043 whites will be 49% of the population.

White supremacy is a worldwide threat now CNN proclaims.

Much of the special was an interview by a white nationalist, Jarod Taylor, who advocates separating the races geographically from each other and establishing a white only nation as part of the geography of the United States. This guy in no way shape or form is representative of white people in the United States yet he is held up as the representative by CNN. This is a disgusting tactic by CNN to paint white people in this country with the disgusting views of this one white nationalist idiot. This is a purposeful and malevolent distortion of white people in our country for the purposes of sowing the seeds of fear and distrust among the people in our country that are not white.

I find this tactic to be a snake slithering out of the mouth of Fareed Zakaria. Frankly this CNN host should be ashamed of himself using this dishonest tactic against all of us white people. During the interview with this crazy white nationalist, Fareed Zakaria asked him about the IQ differences between different races. This is an uncomfortable truth new to many people that is upsetting. There have been multiple studies conducted by different scientists that show there is some systemic differences. Some Jewish people have the highest IQ among humans, sub-Saharan blacks have the lowest on average. Individuals do indeed vary. Jarod Taylor said this. Fareed then showed us that all humans share 99.9% of the same DNA as if to say what Taylor said is scientifically false. Well, no. The DNA example has nothing to do with IQ really. But Fareed is dishonest enough not to say that and use it as so called "proof", which it is not.

Worse, another study has been done by one of the people that mapped the human genome. He said, *"There is no basis in scientific fact or in the human genetic code for the notion that skin color will be predictive of intelligence".* Well of course. This applies to individuals and not large groups of people where averages are needed. Everyone does have slightly different DNA. So, what this scientist said is true but does not apply to the study of large groups of people. But again, his statement was willfully and purposely misused by CNN and Fareed Zakaria to promote his story that whites are villains and it is getting worse. Just not true. They lied again.

Furthering the same tactic CNN used the Oklahoma City bombing as proof of white supremacy in this country. Never mind that the motivation for that horrific bloody bombing was against our government. It was a government building is blown up.

"in 1993. McVeigh claimed that the building in Oklahoma City was targeted to avenge the more than 70 deaths at Waco."

"Motivated by his dislike for the U.S. federal government and unhappy about its handling of the Ruby Ridge incident in 1992 and the Waco siege in 1993, McVeigh timed his attack to coincide with the second anniversary of the deadly fire that ended the siege at the Branch Davidian compound in Waco, Texas.[12][13]"

But CNN paints the lying false picture that Timothy McVeigh was a racist and therefore the bombing was racist. CNN claimed that a book called the Turner diaries was his favorite and the motivation for the Oklahoma City bombing. No other source I could find has made the same false claim, only CNN. They go on to paint the author of "The Turner Diaries" as a malevolent monster who wanted to blow up cities with atomic bombs. However, McVeigh was a member of the Patriot movement which denied the legitimacy of the federal government and law enforcement. The attack was against our federal government. The attack was against the Alfred P. Murrah Federal Building.

CNN lies about this to produce a false and fake narrative against white people. So, who are the real racists? If you lie about race in order to produce fear against the white race, then you are a racist. CNN can only be described by this falsification as a racist entity promoting racism against whites. Fareed Zakaria is also a racist for the very same reason why falsifying willfully and purposely the motive behind the Oklahoma City bombing and calling it a racist action against people of color by a white man. It was not. I personally condemn both CNN and Fareed Zakaria for doing this and selling Satan's seeds fear, hate and distrust within our great country.

And they do all of these lies under the guise of so-called legitimate journalism. Satan is the author of all lies and deceit. It is obvious to this pastoral minister that Satan has found a comfortable home at the headquarters of CNN and in the minds of many of its so-called journalists who are in fact only propaganda ministers, propaganda of hate, lies, misinformation and innuendo to support the false narrative that white people are on the march in order to crush immigrants of a different color. That accusation is disgusting and blatantly false.

Summary:

Are there white supremacists in America? YES! Are they rotten people? Yes! But CNN has taken an existing problem and blown it way out of proportion in this writer's opinion. They have constructed an image that there is a white bogey man at every corner. Just not true, but to watch their video you would think so.

CNN is a vile hateful source of liberal and racist lies. The propaganda hit job against white people documented here is a prime example of how we cannot believe CNN or other mainstream media outlets. They do have a political agenda which is to usher into the United States political change where the masses of people can be easily controlled by a few mega wealthy people through intimidation and force, just like China is doing today. Their preferred tool is socialism.

It is actually easy it is to uncover the truth and expose the Satanically driven purveyors of hate, lies of both omission and commission, destructive innuendos and false narratives in order to sow the seeds of destruction between the existing loving connections the American people already enjoy between each other. It is CNN and people like Fareed Zakaria that are the real and rabid racists in our country for it is they who promote racism by sowing the seeds of fear among us all. Resist them by simply tuning into a different channel and let them collapse into the dust from which they came. And pray to God for guidance.

In my opinion, the entire Democrat Party has given itself over to Satanic hate of God's children. Look at the four horsewomen of the apocalypse called "The Squad". Each of these women have no understanding of Judeo-Christian principles and how that forms a rock solid foundation for mankind to prosper in a manner ordained by Almighty God.

Ilham Omar is a dedicated Muslim and one of the four horsewomen. She has no gratefulness in her heart for being accepted into American society from Somalia. Rather she outwardly hates this American nation by all the terrible things she says, she condones, and she promotes.

"Omar's continual demonization of Israel and anti-Semitic rhetoric has been a central theme of her many controversial views. In 2012, Omar tweeted, "Israel has hypnotized the world, may Allah awaken the people and help them see the evil doings of Israel." [117] This hate speech is typical of Muslims against anything in the Christian western world. Yet, there she is in congress spewing hatred toward Jews and Christians, and we hear NOTHING from the Democrat Party leadership about her hate speech. Nope. Yes, this is highly hypocritical.

---

[117] Conservative Daily News, Amalia White,

"Omar recently introduced a House resolution that "affirms" Americans' purported "right" to engage in the anti-Semitic Boycott, Divestment, and Sanctions (BDS) campaign that pursues the ultimate elimination of the world's only Jewish state."

Richard Ferguson

Richard Ferguson is available for book interviews and personal appearances. For more information contact:

Richard Ferguson
C/O Advantage Books
P.O. Box 160847
Altamonte Springs, FL 32716
info@advbooks.com

Other books by Richard Furguson:

Christians Alert! Democrats are attacking our country	ISBN: 978-1-59755-525-8
The Children of the Swamp	ISBN: 978-1-59755-545-6

To purchase additional copies of these books, visit our bookstore at:
www.advbookstore.com

*A*dvantage
BOOKS

Longwood, Florida, USA
"we bring dreams to life"™
www.advbookstore.com

www.ingramcontent.com/pod-product-compliance
Lightning Source LLC
Chambersburg PA
CBHW072143270326
41931CB00010B/1866

* 9 7 8 1 5 9 7 5 5 5 4 8 7 *